Al-Qalam Journal

of Advanced Islamic Research

Issue 2

AL-QALAM JOURNAL
OF ADVANCED ISLAMIC RESEARCH

International Centre *for* Advanced
Islamic Research (ICAIR)

AL-QALAM JOURNAL
OF ADVANCED ISLAMIC RESEARCH

Al-Qalam Journal

ISSN 2755-3698

ISBN PAPERBACK: 978-1-78991-177-0

ISBN HARDBACK: 978-1-78991-176-3

ISBN DIGITAL COPY: 978-1-78991-178-7

VOLUME 1 • ISSUE 2

International Centre *for* Advanced Islamic Research (ICAIR)
www.icair.ac
qalamjournal@world-federation.org

Transliteration

Arabic has been transliterated according to the following key:

ء	ʾ	ض	ḍ
ا	a	ط	ṭ
ب	b	ظ	ẓ
ت	t	ع	ʿ
ث	th	غ	gh
ج	j	ف	f
ح	ḥ	ق	q
خ	kh	ك	k
د	d	ل	l
ذ	dh	م	m
ر	r	ن	n
ز	z	ه	h
س	s	و	w
ش	sh	ي	y
ص	ṣ	ة	a; at in *iḍāfah*

Vowels and Diphthongs

ـَا	ā	ـَوْ	aw
ـُو	ū	ـَيْ	ay
ـِي	ī		
ـَ	a		
ـُ	u		
ـِ	i		

Contents

بِسْمِ اللَّهِ الرَّحْمَٰنِ الرَّحِيمِ

Editorial Foreword

The Inspiration

The title of this journal (Al-Qalam) is inspired by Qur'anic teachings. I wish to first elaborate how this term was interpreted by the Ahl al-Bayt, and why this special term was chosen for this journal.

What is al-qalam? The Philosophy of the Qur'anic oath

The term *al-qalam* – which literally means "the pen" – is mentioned in the Qur'an in Sūrat al-Qalam, which was revealed in Mecca (although some interpreters disagree as to whether some of its verses were revealed in Mecca or Medina).

This chapter begins: "*Nūn*. By the pen and whatever they write ..." (Q 66:1). This first letter is an example of the mystical single letters that are scattered throughout the Qur'an, such as *Yā Sīn* amongst others. These mystical letters have been interpreted to sometimes refer to one of the secret names of Prophet Muḥammad, and sometimes preceding oaths by sacred entities, such as in this chapter where it swears by the Prophet himself, "By the pen and by whatever they write", thereafter declaring that he is not insane. Hence, the chapter starts with these items to assure that the content is extremely important and crucial, as it is swearing to emphasise that the Holy Prophet is not insane, and also providing us with the correct formula to measure sanity and distinguish it from insanity.

However, there is another interpretation of the verses in a tradition that is narrated by Fayḍ al-Kāshānī in his exegesis titled *al-Ṣāfī*, that: "[Al-Ṣadūq in his book, *Ma'ānī al-akhbār*], has narrated from Sufyān from the authority of Imam Ja'far al-Ṣādiq that he told him: '*Nūn* was a river in heaven, and the Lord ordered it to become solid, so it became solid. Then it became the ink to the pen, so the Lord ordered the pen to write. Thus it has written whatever is included in the tablet (*lawḥ maḥfūẓ*), which contains whatever is existing or going to exist until the Day of Judgement. As such, *nūn* is the ink of light, and the pen is the pen of light, while the tablet is the tablet of light.' Then Sufyān approached Imam al-Ṣādiq saying: 'O son of the Holy Prophet, can you elaborate further as to what these are: *nūn*, the pen, and the tablet? O Imam, teach from whatever you have been taught!' The Imam replied: 'O Ibn Saʿīd, if you were not a qualified companion I would have never revealed these secrets to you! Indeed, *nūn* is an angel, who is reporting to the pen, who in turn is also an angel. The pen is reporting to the tablet, who is an angel, and he reports to the angel Isrāfīl, who then reports to the angel Mīkāʾīl, who is to report to the archangel Jibrīl, who is finally to report to all the divine messengers and prophets. O Ibn Saʿīd, I am afraid that this amount of information is too extensive for you, so go and keep it secretive!'"

Based on the implication of this narration, one is led to conclude that there are six angels involved, three of them are strictly entrusted with knowledge, while other three of them – who are at the top of the hierarchy – are all involved in reporting the required details of knowledge to the prophets. The pen is the middle stage in this ascending chain of knowledge, and most certainly crucial in its functionality and dynamical knowledge production. As such the Prophet cannot be considered insane, rather those who speak without evidence and/or illogically in an inconsistent manner – due to being ill-informed or ignorant – are indeed the insane.

Being inspired by this Qur'anic yet technical term (the pen), one is humbly not claiming to bear this honour, i.e. being the pen, but rather just reflecting the aspiration for which one shall struggle, i.e. bridging the gulf between the centres of knowledge production – the Ḥawza ʿIlmiyya of Shīʿa Muslims – and western academia.

Distinctive Features: Differentiating between two Educational Systems

As this journal aims to bridge the gulf between western academia and the Ḥawza centres, one is inclined to explain about the Ḥawza and its differences with universities.

Firstly, one ought to emphasise that the Ḥawza of Najaf was founded in 449/1057 by Shaykh al-Ṭā'ifa, Muḥammad b. al-Ḥasan al-Ṭūsī, who settled in Najaf in 449/1057, and who had to escape rampant sectarian sedition initiated by the Seljuks in Baghdad.

This historical fact implies that this system outdates the earliest globally known university, i.e. in Bologna, Italy, in 1088 CE. Furthermore, it implies that this very elevated Shīʿī figure (Muḥammad b. al-Ḥasan al-Ṭūsī) was himself involved in establishing scientific circles as well as the technicalities related to their groundbreaking formation. He was known for his oceanic knowledge being an affluent thinker in theology, jurisprudence, and the exegesis of the Qur'an. He is also known to be the author of two major Shīʿī compilations of hadith, *Tahdhīb al-aḥkām* and *al-Istibṣār*, which is known by its innovative style, having established the fundamental trends amongst Shīʿī Muslims to re-examine any narration before accepting its authenticity.

After that he wrote two extensive works on the comparative approach between Shīʿī and Sunnī jurisprudence (*al-Khilāf*), and the innovative and detailed production of Islamic demonstrative jurisprudence (*al-Mabsūṭ*). He was the first Shīʿī scholar to have written on the principles of Islamic jurisprudence in his famous book, *al-ʿUddah*. In addition, he is known for his extensive exegesis of the Qur'an (*al-Tibyān*), and also his excellent works on the bibliography of Shīʿī books (*al-Fihrist*), and corrective methodology regarding the narrators of hadith (*Ikhtiyār maʿrifat al-rijāl*).

Based on those historical contributions he was, in fact, the first scholar who established Shīʿī thoughts, methodologies, their fundamental principles, and presented their foundations that are still espoused by the centres of knowledge.

As there are many differences between the two intellectual systems, I intend only to highlight and emphasise the important ones. I shall try to demonstrate this within a historical context, but in addition to the analysis of the available data.

A Contribution from Historical Developments in the Modern History

Even though both Ḥawza and universities are serving their relevant societies, their development is entirely dissimilar. Within Europe, the universities were presented and built on already established, classical religious institutions. This has contributed to their positive growth. However, in the East and/or Muslim world, the academic centres were presented parallel to, and in competition with, the classical religious [*madrasah*] Ḥawza.

It would be superficial to claim that both educational institutions were introduced to accomplish each other, or even to standardise their methodologies of research. The universities were presented to approach knowledge in a secular European style, and to be mainly inclined to study science and modern technology that are related to the material and worldly life. It was also introduced to indirectly challenge -what they wrongly claimed- the "primitive" minds of traditional religious institutions.

It is, therefore, Muslim scholars who have had suspicious reactions and defensive and negative responses to this newly presented educational system. Even in the twenty-first century one encounters this, and one tries to address it. I believe that these tragic results could have been avoided if one were smarter in the introduction and implementation of the modern educational system.

It is -in fact- the task of the International Centre for Advanced Islamic Research (ICAIR), to bridge the gulf between the two educuation systems. However, ICAIR aspires that this Al-Qalam journal, which seeks to abide by strict academic standards, will be a constructive channel for exchange and dialogue between intellectuals and scholars from both traditional Islamic and academic backgrounds.

Contributing to the Al-Qalam Journal: Policies and Conditions

The Al-Qalam Journal aims to address issues pertaining to the needs of the academic milieu, fulfilling current requirements. These issues should pertain to Islamic studies and the constructive principles of knowledge production.

Following the legacy of the classical Shīʿī seminary and its production, we promote innovative and objective research that has direct or indirect practical application. Therefore, Al-Qalam will publish articles that comprise of new research, reviews of current books, and opinions from affluent thinkers who work diligently to pave the way for establishing the foundation for applied research and innovative ideas which contribute to the global Islamic civilisation.

Some of our articles are originally papers that were presented in international academic conferences or stand-alone topics. Many articles in the first edition were dedicated to the topic of exaggeration (*ghuluww*). All contributions are welcome as long as they meet the required academic standards and fulfil the aims of the journal.

Any submitted article must not have been published previously nor be under consideration for publication elsewhere. Like many journals, Al-Qalam follows a two-blind review process, and if a submission is accepted, it shall be requested to follow our transliteration and referencing style before being published.

We employ a strict embargo policy, where reporting an article and its findings by the media is embargoed until a specified time.

Ali H. Al-Hakim, Guest Editor, Al-Qalam
(Ijtihād) (Cand.Mag.) (PhD) (DProf)

Al-Qalam Journal

ACADEMIC ARTICLES

Reflections on Duʿāʾ al-Bahāʾ (al-Saḥar)

Ali H. Al-Hakim

Senior Research Fellow, ICAIR, London

ABSTRACT

This article will demonstrate the importance of a well-known supplication to be read during the nights of the holy month of Ramaḍān, known by the names Du'ā' al-Bahā' and Du'ā' al-Saḥar. It is formulated in a unique and special way, as the supplicant first calls upon the Almighty by His utmost and highest attributes, so as to correct and remind himself that all of Allah's attributes are to be characterised equally. Taking a critical look at the text leads one to question the philosophy of its style and to ask what reminder it intends to give the wayfarer or anyone else who reads it, or how one can be assured that this supplication is backed by the technical principles of hadith and accepted authentication methods. This article will explain that this supplication is unique and rich in information that could only have been issued and inspired by the Shī'ī Imams.

KEYWORDS: Reflecting the Beauty – Divine Attributes – Supplication – Divine Interaction – Qur'anic Monotheism – Du'ā' Saḥar – Its Authenticity

Introduction

Du'ā' al-Bahā' (al-Saḥar) consists of the elements of both supplication (*du'ā'*) and invocation (*tawassul*), interspersed with reminders for the self as to the proper method by which to gain deep knowledge of Allah. In twenty-one parts, this supplication gives the petitioner the opportunity to mediate with Allah at the time of *saḥar* (pre-dawn, early morning). Some of the invocations call on Allah by a particular divine name or attribute and end with that aspect of Him that is most encompassing and comprehensive; for example: "O Allah, I do entreat You by Your authority and omnipotence!" A quick comparison of the first to the penultimate invocations, however, shows that the prayer begins with the more specific attributes of Allah and continues by reminding the reader that Allah's words are utterly complete and that His power is all-prevailing before moving on to invoking a more universal and absolute divine attribute, for example by saying: "O Allah, I do entreat You by all of Your words!" or: "O Allah, I do entreat You by all of Your power!"

From another angle, if we were to compare the twenty-first (and final) invocation we will see that it calls on Allah by one of His characteristics that is almost completely opposite to the one used in the first invocation. The final invocation suggests a movement from the universal, back to the particular. The supplicant begins by saying: "O Allah, I do entreat You by Your authority and omnipotence!" This description of God is absolute and universal. Gradually, then, the supplicant becomes more specific, saying: "I entreat You by each and every one of Your works and powers, one by one!" The supplicant concludes by invoking the Lord of lords and the All-Sovereign.

This article comprises two sections; the first discusses lessons to be learned from the supplication, followed by a comparison of Islamic teachings and Western thought in this field. The second section re-examines the authenticity of this supplication.

Section One

Lessons from the Supplication

There are three subtle lessons to be drawn from this supplication: one is spiritual, another is doctrinal, and the third and final one is to do with mystical metaphysics.

The Spiritual Lesson

The first lesson from this supplication is spiritual. One who is journeying to their Lord must carefully ponder the words of Duʿāʾ Abū Ḥamza al-Thumālī: "I knew You through You, You guided me to You, You called me to You, and were it not for You, I would not know anything about You."

On one hand, one might turn to Allah in supplication because He is the proper destination of supplications. The Qur'an says: "Call on Me and I will answer you" (Q 40:60). This verse clearly enjoins people to supplicate to Allah. This is what Duʿāʾ Abū Ḥamza refers to when it says: "You called me to You," as the purpose of supplication is not to satisfy the ego of the one being called upon, but rather to look after the needs of the one who calls out, and to fulfil their legitimate desires. At the same time, however, it is also an expression of humility and a plea, for the supplicant sees that he must invoke Allah with His best and nearest qualities to his own heart, and His most perfect attributes according to the supplicant's own understanding and comprehension. Therefore, he humbly entreats Allah by His greatest attributes – His most-pervasive knowledge, His most-comprehensive names, and His all-extensive power.

It is then that the supplicant becomes aware that He only knows Allah according to his own limited understanding rather than as Allah truly is in terms of His absolute knowledge and absolute power, as all of God's attributes are absolute and none are limited. Thus, the supplicant comes to grasp a more comprehensive understanding of divine unity in accordance with the Qur'an, which encompasses the teachings of all the prophets and messengers. Hence, the supplicant returns to Allah again, this time with the knowledge that all of Allah's knowledge is all-pervasive, all of His power is all-extensive, and so on. He invokes Allah "by all of Your knowledge" and "by all of Your power."

When the supplicant reaches the twenty-first part of the supplication, they have gone from spiritually travelling towards Allah to spiritually travelling in Allah. The former state has an end and a limit, which Imam Zayn al-ʿĀbidīn describes in Duʿāʾ Abū Ḥamza thusly: "For surely the wayfarer towards You is near in distance, and You are not veiled from them, but their deeds veil them from You!"

On the other hand, travelling in Allah is without end or limit, as described by Mullā ʿAbd al-Razzāq al-Kāshānī.[1]

This journeying in Allah is without limit, and the supplicant will realise that they are standing before the Absolute, whose knowledge is all-permeating, whose power is all-pervading, and whose names are complete. Thereat, they will be overcome by divine bounties and lordly blessings, recalling the verses: "And as for your Lord's blessing, proclaim it!" (Q 93:11); "So which of your Lord's bounties will you both deny?" (Q55:13); and "If the sea were ink for the words of my Lord, the sea would be spent before the words of my Lord were spent" (Q 18:109).

After traversing the lines of this wonderful formulation of expression linked to one's deeds and beliefs, it becomes apparent to the spiritual traveller that travelling to their Lord, travelling with their self, and travelling with their Lord and their self together must lead them to becoming a "wayfarer without a wayfarer" such that they do not see themself as existing except on the level of spiritual annihilation (*fanāʾ*), about which the verse says: "And you did not throw when you threw, rather it was Allah who threw" (Q 8:17). In a similar vein, it is transmitted from Imam al-Ṣādiq: "It is as though I heard it from the One who spoke it!"[2]

The Doctrinal Lesson

Another lesson to be learned from this supplication is a doctrinal one.

---

[1] ʿAbd al-Razzāq Kāshānī, *Muʿjam iṣṭilāḥāt al-Ṣūfiyya*, v. 2, p. 31.

[2] Ibn Ṭāwūs, *Falāḥ al-sāʾil*, p. 107. He narrates that the Imam would pray and recite the Qur'an in his prayer until he lost consciousness. When he regained consciousness, someone would ask: "What caused this state to befall you?" He would answer: "I recited the verse until I reached the state in which I heard it directly as it was revealed."

In each part of the supplication, the supplicant begins by invoking that which he, in his limited understanding, believes to be the best and most perfect. However, on the subject of Allah's power, he invokes it again by recalling that there is no differentiation within Allah's power, as all instances of it are omnipotent. Equally, the supplicant recalls that all of Allah's splendour is splendorous, and all of His words are complete. We, in our limited and deficient understanding, see things from just one angle rather than in their totality. Hence, the supplicant goes back and invokes Allah by His most absolute attribute – after all, does not Allah say of Himself that He is the First, the Last, the Outer, and the Inner? Hence, he says: "O Allah, I do entreat You by all of Your power!" and: "I do entreat You by all of Your words!" and so on.[3]

This does not mean, of course, that the supplicant has erred and corrected himself. Rather, what we see in this supplication is an ascent towards a broader, more comprehensive, and more complete understanding of Allah, one that distinguishes the teachings of Islam as brought to mankind by the Noble Messenger. In his commentary on the *Fuṣūṣ* of Ibn ʿArabī, al-Qayṣarī says about Prophet Muḥammad: "His is the wisdom of singularity because he is the most perfect creation of humankind, for which reason the whole affair begins and ends. He was a prophet when Adam was still between water and the clay, and he is, by his elemental makeup, the Seal of the Prophets, first of the three singular ones, as all other singulars derive from it. He was the clearest of evidence for his Lord, having been given the totality of the divine words."[4]

In his commentary on this passage, al-Qayṣarī writes: "He was the most perfect creation of humankind, because the prophets – may Allah's blessings be upon all of them – were the most perfect creations of this species, and each of them is a locus of manifestation for a universal divine name (*ism kullī*), and all of these universal names are

[3] See an extensive explanation to this *duʿā'* by Ayatollah Maẓāhirī: https://shorturl.at/qHR04, accessed on 29.08.2023.

[4] Ibn ʿArabī, *The Bezels of Wisdom*, trans. R. W. J. Austin, p. 272.

subsumed beneath the divine name of which [the Prophet] is the locus of manifestation. Therefore, he is the most perfect member of this species, and because he is the most perfect member of this species, the affair of creation began with the origination of his spirit first and ended with the affair of his divine mission last. He is the archetype of Adam in the origination, and it is he who manifests the archetype of the finality of the species."

This is not restricted to the Prophet being the seal of divine law (*sharīʿa*) alone, but encompasses everything that he brought in his message: ideas, laws, doctrines, and ethics. He said: "I have been sent only to complete the most noble of morals (*makārim al-akhlāq*)." Meanwhile, the Qur'an says through the Prophet: "Today I have perfected your religion for you, and I have completed My blessing upon you, and I have approved Islam as your religion" (Q 5:3).[5]

The Metaphysical Lesson

I find myself compelled to elevate the present research to a more advanced level, rather than simple pantheism and deity metaphysics, perhaps to pure panentheism, because the divine names and attributes invoked in this supplication occur in comparison with one another and are arranged in order of precedence. How should this be done? The answer to this question will be even more lucid once we have processed the ideas within the doctrinal and spiritual lessons.

In the preliminary discussions of his commentary on the *Fuṣūṣ* of Ibn ʿArabī, and after explaining what will become of the unseen on the Day of the Greater Resurrection, al-Qayṣarī says: "He will cause things to pass into nothingness during the Greater Resurrection by becoming manifest in His oneness (*waḥda*) and overwhelming them by removing their individualities and qualities and rendering them evanescent, as per the verses: 'To whom does the sovereignty belong today? To God, the One, the All-paramount!' (Q 40:16), and 'Everything is to perish

[5] This is based on my explanatory text to *Sharḥ Fuṣūṣ* of Ibn ʿArabī, by al-Qayṣarī.

except His face' (Q 28:88).

"On the Lesser Resurrection, He will move from the realm of the visible to the realm of the unseen, or from one form to another in a single realm. Insofar as these are the forms of His entelechies and the manifestations of His names and attributes, they manifest first in knowledge (*'ilm*) and then in entity (*'ayn*) according to His desire to make manifest His signs and demonstrate His will. Thus they will multiply according to their forms, while He remains unchanged in His real sempiternal oneness. He comprehends the realities of things as He comprehends the reality of His own essence, not through some other means such as the First Intellect (*al-'aql al-awwal*), because those realities are also identical with His essence in reality (*ḥaqīqa*), even while they differ from it in entification (*ta'ayyun*).

"No one else comprehends Him, as per the verses: 'Human vision does not encompass Him, yet He encompasses human sight' (Q 6:103); 'but they cannot comprehend Him in their knowledge' (Q 20:11); 'They do not regard Allah with the regard due to Him' (Q 6:91); and 'Allah warns you to beware of Him' (Q 3:30). Allah admonishes His servants out of His sympathy and mercy for them, lest they squander their lives pursuing that which they can never obtain. If one understands that all existence (*wujūd*) is the Reality (*al-ḥaqq*), then one can know the secret behind His words: 'and He is with you wherever you may be' (Q 57:4); 'and We are nearer to him than you are, though you do not perceive' (Q 56:85); '... and in your souls. Will you not then perceive?' (Q 51:21); 'It is He who is Allah in the sky and Allah on the earth' (Q 43:84); 'Allah is the Light of the heavens and the earth' (Q 24:35); 'He indeed comprehends all things' (Q 41:54); and an *al-ḥadīth al-qudsī*: 'And I was his hearing and his sight.'[6] One can also know the secret of the Prophet's saying: 'If you

[6] *Al-ḥadīth al-qudsī* narrations are the words of the Almighty, not stemming from the Qur'an but rather narrated by the Prophet. This particular hadith is narrated in *Ṣaḥīḥ al-Bukhārī* (v. 5, p. 2384), and by the Sunni sources *Musnad Aḥmad ibn Ḥanbal* and *Sunan al-Bayhaqī*; see *Fatḥ al-bārī fī sharḥ al-Bukhārī*, narration 6502. One may also read it in *Sharḥ al-ḥikam al-ghawthiyya*, p. 45 (by

were to lower a rope, it would land on Allah,'[7] as well as the secrets of other sayings like this that draw you towards true monotheism (*tawḥīd*) through allusive language."

After expounding some of the attributes of the Necessary Being, al-Qayṣarī examines how He was invoked by the prophets and that He has the most beautiful names. Al-Qayṣarī has tried to elaborate on these names and on the fact that from Him is the origin and to Him is the return. After expounding on how He is described in the words of the prophets, in the words of beauty and perfection, and the phrase "He is with you wherever you are" – "with" here being used in the sense of ontological sustaining (*qayyūmiyya*), "Allah, there is no god except Him, the Living One, the All-sustaining" (Q 2:255) – al-Qayṣarī shows that neither the human being nor anything else possesses any special qualities. Humankind began by His word, marking His fixity as an individuated entity, not merely His simultaneity, and that is because what is meant by identity (*ʿayniyya*) does not contradict alterity (*ghayriyya*). If He is a boundless existence (*mawjūd muṭlaq*), however, then He is both self and other. Therefore, identity and alterity exist together as complementary opposites, not as contradictory elements. In other words, that to which is referred in this context as the most beautiful names and their unseen equivalents complement the visible ones.

Allah is both the Manifest and the Hidden. That is what the Commander of the Faithful and Master of the Monotheists, Imam ʿAlī referred to when he said: "He is within things but not through mixing,

---

Abū Midyan Shuʿayb b. Ḥasan al-Tilmisānī al-Maghribī, published by Dār al-Āfāq al-ʿArabiyya, Cairo: 2008). It is also narrated by Shīʿī sources, see *al-Kāfī*, v. 2, p. 253, narrations 7 and 8.

[7] This is a narration that was transmitted by al-Tirmidhī, from Ḥasan al-Baṣrī, from Abū Hurayra. It is not authenticated in accordance with the principles of knowledge related to narrators of hadith, as it is unclear how Ḥasan al-Baṣrī could narrate from Abū Hurayra when their lives were separated by a long period of time.

and outside them but not through separation."[8] Through reflection, one may see that he is referring to the divine reflection post-creation.

There is also a hidden and unseen aspect that is not complemented by a manifest one, and this is the level of divine unicity (*maqām al-aḥadiyya*). Then there is alterity unmatched by identity, and this, too, is the station of unicity that is above the level of the First (*maqām al-awwal*).

Allah the Almighty says that He is absolute manifestation (*al-ẓuhūr al-muṭlaq*), the meaning of which was explained prior to this section. The absolute manifestation has no complementary opposite; Allah is the absolute manifestation, which is the station of the divine essence (*maqām al-dhāt*) that has no complementary opposite. Other narrations have referred to it as the absolutely unknown (*amma*),[9] in accordance with Prophet Muḥammad's answer, when he was approached about the divinity in this stage.

Were we to descend from the level of the divine essence to the level of entification (*maqām al-taʿayyun*), insofar as our discussion is about the station of the essence of the unseen (*maqām dhāt al-ghayb*) (as a full negation, not as an affirmative proposition in negative form or a full affirmation), by "pure unseen" or "the unseen of the unseen" is not meant the "unseen" merely in the sense of "not visible" but also in the sense of "totally unseen". At the level of entification, however, there are two identical existences. If one were to say: "There is the unseen and the visible," and "These are the unseen and the visible," they are one and the same, because this is a level beneath that of the divine essence.

Sometimes, we might say "there is the unseen" without anything being there to complement it, and this is the unseen at the level of the divine essence, which is without entification or opposite. As for

[8] See *Nahj al-balāgha*, sermon 150, which begins: "All thanks belongs to Allah, who has manifested Himself through His creation."

[9] This narration has been transmitted in *Sunan Ibn Māja* and *Sunan al-Bayhaqī*, as well as by *al-Tirmidhī* in his *Sunan*, who considered it authenticated and/or described it to be "good" just like al-Dhahabī.

the unseen that exists at the level of visibility (*maqām al-shahāda*), meaning the hidden (*al-bāṭin*) that is the opposite of the manifest (*al-ẓāhir*), they are entifications that are sometimes expressed as "hidden and manifest" and sometimes as "unseen and visible". All of these are entifications which exist only when we descend from the level of the Highest of the high, meaning the Absolutely Unseen in the sense of a simple negation (not in the sense of an affirmation by way of negation or a full affirmation), for at this level, He exists without predication or entification, and there is no opposite for Him. When we descend to the lowest level, which is that of manifestation, there is entification, and insofar as entification occurs, it can be divided into the categories of manifest, hidden, visible, and unseen. These four divine names all occur under the name of "the Absolutely Manifest" (*al-ẓāhir al-muṭlaq*), which is without opposite.

Therefore, talking about "He is the First and the Last, the Manifest and the Hidden" entails our descent to a third level, which means restraining ourselves from the level of the Absolutely Unseen (*al-ghayb al-muṭlaq*), which takes the form of a simple negation, our descent to the level of the Absolutely Manifest, which is the level of entification, and to the level of the entifications of the unseen, the visible, the manifest, and the hidden.

Therefore, as you can see, the question is not resolved, and the commentator has dealt with it in a disorganised fashion. How can those things exist at the level of entification when He says: "He is the First and the Last, the Manifest and the Hidden?" In reality, the commentator has said that He is not things without bringing any evidence to support this claim! Therefore, it is an attempt at a response, but the commentator has not done the topic justice. He provides no evidence for Him being other than things; instead, he has satisfied himself with referring to Qur'anic verses without delving into any arguments.

In fact, to rephrase the same using a theological concept and recorded narration, one may refer to the time when Imam ʿAlī was approached about the term "face of Allah" (*wajh allāh*) and said that he could not describe it; instead, he implemented a physical, albeit very convenient example. He ordered a fire to be lit, and then asked the enquirer as to where the face of the fire was. The answer was, of course, "The fire has different faces, depending on which angle one would like to observe it. Also it is almost inaccessible, as it is continuously and constantly changing!" Thus the Imam concluded that the fire was metaphorically synonymous with the face of Allah, the Almighty.

What is meant in the Qur'anic verse by the face of a deity or the "countenance of Allah"?

J. Seydanloo and M. Karaminia wrote in an article on the subject that they believe the term "countenance" in the Holy Qur'an has several meanings, the highest of which is attributed to Allah. A correct understanding of the meaning of "Allah's countenance" like other divine names and attributes, plays a great role in creating a true monotheistic belief in Allah. Misunderstanding its correct interpretation will cause fault in belief, and polytheism in belief and practice.

For example, some commentators suggest a material and physical interpretation of Allah's countenance, relying on the apparent meaning of the verses; some do not interpret such verses, and others interpret them as the divine essence, His attributes, divine will and satisfaction, as well as prophets and divine authorities. One must deal with the semantics of Allah's countenance in contemporary exegeses, presenting the perspective of some contemporary philosophers of metaphysics, and conclude from the evidence with this point of view that the essence of Allah is not visible to any creature.

One should be able to imply the verse of "and whither so ever ye turn, there is Allah's countenance"[10] and the illusion of death and destruction also has no place in it to seek exemption from "Everything will perish save His countenance."[11] Based on that, one may conclude that "the countenance of Allah" actually means His attributes and revelations,

---

[10] See Q 2:115.

[11] See Q 28:88.

the highest examples of which are the prophets and the Shīʿī Imams. ʿAllāma Ḥillī reports that it is narrated from Ḥamīd b. al-Muthannā, who narrated from Imam al-Bāqir:

قال إن الله خلو من خلقه وخلقه خلو منه

> "God does not contain His creation, and His creation does not contain Him."[12]

Despite the fact that the Almighty is reflected in His creation, there is a clear distinction between Him and His creation, such that He cannot be described in the same way His creations are described, nor the other way round.

It is also narrated from Imam ʿAlī:

بان من الأشياء بالقهر لها والقدرة عليها، وبانت الأشياء منه بالخضوع له والرجوع إليه

> "He is to be distinguished from His creation through His omnipotent power over them; and they are distinguished from Him through being in total need of Him and humbled before Him."[13]

With this narration one may be able to grasp the exact meaning of the interpretation of al-Qayṣarī. As the quoted words indicate, there are two aspects of hiddenness: the first belongs to the divine essence, and the other belongs to the divine manifestations (*maẓāhir*). That is why Allah attributes hiddenness to Himself at the level of the divine attributes (*maqām al-ṣifa*) and sometimes at the level of the divine acts (*maqām al-fiʿl*). According to the principles of metaphysics, His attributes cover everything, because He has mastery over everything; hence, He must be other than everything, because He has control over everything. This alterity is an opposite attribute to identity.

Then there is alterity at the level of the divine acts, or hiddenness

---

[12] Al-Ṣadūq, *Kitāb al-tawḥīd*, v. 1, p. 105; al-Kulaynī, *al-Kāfī*, v. 1, p. 82.

[13] See *Sharḥ Mullā Ṣāliḥ al-Māzandarānī*, at https://bit.ly/3zppyoi, accessed on 25.07.2022.

at the level of action, which exists beneath the divine names of *al-shāfī* (the Healer) and *al-kāfī* (the Sufficer), and beneath the divine manifestations of *al-mumriḍ* (the One Who Causes Sickness) and *al-rāziq* (the Provider). Therefore, He expounds His own nature at the level of action, and this is what distinguishes this world from the hereafter, or, as we have explained, the lesser resurrection from the greater resurrection. Sometimes, Allah becomes manifest as the Creator and the Provider, and sometimes He becomes manifest as the All-Paramount. He has neither veil nor manifestation in the sense that His attributes overwhelm all other attributes; otherwise, it would make no sense to say that He becomes manifest without any veil.

Clearly, it is difficult to draw a clear distinction between these different levels, so what can the spiritual wayfarer do in this situation but be astonished and give no heed to the perfection with which his Master addresses him, while He exists in His own self on different levels.

Islamic Sources and Western Thinkers

The best elaboration for the Western think tank is produced by the term "panentheism", a word constructed from the Greek terms "pan" meaning all, "en" meaning in, and "theism" derived from the Greek "*theos*" meaning god. As such, panentheism considers "God" and the world to be interrelated, with the world being in God and God being in the world. While panentheism offers an increasingly popular alternative to classical theism, both it and classical theistic systems affirm divine transcendence and immanence. By prioritising the difference between God and the world, however, classical theistic systems reject any influence by the world upon God, while panentheism affirms it.

On the other hand, while pantheism emphasises God's identity with the world, it also maintains the identity and significance of the non-divine, as one has to distinguish between the advanced and elevated status of divinity, but also accept that God is already manifested in His creation. The Stanford Encyclopedia of Philosophy has explained the exact meaning of panentheism by stating:

"Anticipations of panentheistic understandings of God have occurred in both philosophical and theological writings throughout history (Hartshorne and Reese, 1953; J. Cooper, 2006). However, a rich diversity of panentheistic understandings has developed in the past two centuries primarily in Christian traditions responding to scientific thought (Clayton and Peacocke, 2004a).

Although panentheism generally emphasises God's presence in the world without losing the distinct identity of either God or the world, specific forms of panentheism, drawing from different sources, explain the nature of the relationship of God to the world in a variety of ways and come to different conclusions about the nature of the significance of the world for the identity of God.

Panentheists have responded to two primary criticisms: 1) the panentheistic God is a limited God, and 2) panentheism cannot be distinguished from other forms of theism such as classical theism or pantheism ..."[14]

It goes on to distinguish between the various forms of panentheism within Western European notions of it, i.e. the modern term of panentheism has developed through different minds, including German Idealism, Whiteheadian process philosophy, and current scientific thought. Panentheists employ a variety of terms with meanings that are understood by the relevant experts. However, here and now we shall dedicate our discussion about this term from a purely Islamic angle, starting with the words of Isḥāq al-Qūnawī.

The Explanation of a Profound Islamic Pioneer

Muḥammad b. Isḥāq al-Qūnawī, in his *Risālat al-nuṣūṣ*, has given the best explanation of properly distinguishing between the perfection of the divine essence (*al-kamāl al-dhātī*) and that of the divine names (*al-kamāl al-asmā'ī*):

[14] https://plato.stanford.edu/entries/panentheism/, accessed on 25.08.2022.

Naṣṣ on perfection and most-perfectness

"Know that the Real possesses perfection at the level of the divine essence and perfection at the level of the divine names, whose manifestation necessitates the bringing into being of the world, and the two beauties (*al-jamālān*) together with regards to the entification of the two names, because the predication of every predicator, whatever it may be, is preceded by the determination of the thing predicated in the mind of the predicator. Hence, were it not for the cognisance of the essence of the Real before the addition of the divine names to Him and His distinction by virtue of its being without need of anything else for the realisation of its existence, perfection of essence could not be predicated to Him.

There is no doubt that every determination of which the Real is cognisant is a name of His, for surely the names according to the verifying mystic are nothing but the determinations of the Real. After all, every perfection that is attributed to the Real applies to Him as a perfection of the divine names from this angle. With regard to the Real's total absorption in the divine presence of His oneness (*ḥaḍrat waḥdatihi*), which is a corollary of His essence, all of the perfections with which He is described are perfections of His essence.

"Having established this, we say that He has this perfection because of and from His essence, for it is not diminished by external accidents or exigencies at some levels of being in the sense that these do not affect His perfection, and it is impossible to conceive of His perfection admitting any defect in that He is perfect by virtue of it. In fact, some of the accidents and exigencies manifest at some levels of being and operate as qualities of His most-perfectness. One example of this is the knowledge that this is His status."[15]

Mīrzā Hāshim Ishkawarī commented on this with the following: "And know that the conclusion of [al-Qūnawī's] investigation is that the Real is described with contingent attributes and His manifestation according

---

[15] *Risālat al-nuṣūṣ*, pp. 51-52.

to the levels of contingency and, in short, the categorical attachment of contingent attributes to Him. This shows His perfection and most-perfectness because these are signs of His power and attestations of His abounding grace and His all-encompassing providence, such that were He not described with the attribute of one of His manifestations, this would circumscribe the extent of His providence in spite of His transcendence, metaphysical simplicity, and essential lack of need for anything other than Himself. These attributes of His at the level of Himself and fixity (*ithbāt*), demonstrate His attribute of perfection, because they represent the negation of the effects of His not needing anything else and the transcendence of His essence.

On the other hand, from the perspective of realised existence (*thubūt*), they are evidence of His power, tremendousness, and all-encompassing-ness. Therefore, these attributes are neither categorically affirmed for Allah nor categorically denied for Him. On the contrary, it makes sense to affirm them for Him in one or more conditions and negate them in others.

This is a door of knowledge behind which further doors await ... one is that whoever understands this will understand the secret of verses and traditions which might be misread as advocating anthropomorphism (*tashbīh*), such that they do not need interpretation (*ta'wīl*) because their meanings are real with regard to their being manifestations of Allah, nor do they fall within the scope of anthropomorphism, because the Real is transcendent above it with regards to His unseen oneness and His perfect ontological necessity.

The basis for all of this is what He mentioned in the *naṣṣ* ... so ponder and reflect on these, as whatever we have mentioned here we took directly from the words of the Shaykh [Ibn 'Arabī]."[16]

[16] *Ta'līqa bar Risālat al-nuṣūṣ-i Ṣadr al-Dīn-i Qūnawī*, pp. 51-52.

Section Two

Evidence for the Authenticity of the Supplication: Reaching Confidence

It is well known among the experts of hadiths that the supplication is narrated from Imam al-Riḍā and regarded as one of the supplications recited by Imam al-Bāqir at daybreak in the month of Ramaḍān.

Establishing Three Methods

The primary intention of this article is to establish the link between this supplication and the eighth Imam, ʿAlī al-Riḍā, not necessarily as its author, but as the one who informed and/or inspired an individual about its contents.

To establish such link, one of the following three methods could be implemented:

1. quoting actual verifiable historical documents;
2. presenting solid and undisputed testimonies of trustworthy witnesses that the supplication was narrated by reliable narrators; and
3. introducing compelling evidence based on an intertextual and contextual hermeneutical and semantic analysis of the supplication text. Without a doubt, and more preferably, a combination of all three methods, or at least an amalgamation of two of them (i.e. the second and third), should serve our cause in a much stronger way.

The First Method

My claim is that the supplication did appear in an ancient source of hadith, namely one by Ibn Ṭāwūs, who was an expert in the field of prayers and supplications. It was later recorded and further narrated in the encyclopaedia of hadiths, *Biḥār al-anwār,* by the late ʿAllāma al-Majlisī. It is not claimed that this proof reaches the level of a thorough and undisputed assessment of a historical testimony of witnesses; however, Shaykh al-Ṭūsī narrated the supplication from the book *Miṣbāḥ al-mutahajjid,* from which Ibn Ṭāwūs recorded and narrated this supplication in his book, *Iqbāl al-aʿmāl.* Other well-known scholars at later stages wrote extensively on the interpretation of its elevated teachings, for example, M. Qāsim Khalkhālī (who lived during the 13th century AH);[17] Mullā Ḥabīb Kāshānī (1340 AH);[18] Mullā Ḥusayn Tawīsarkānī (1286 AH);[19] the author of *Qiṣaṣ al-ʿulamā',* M. b. Sulaymān al-Tankābunī (1304 AH); M. Ṣāliḥ Māzandarānī Ḥā'irī (1391 AH); Mullā Hidāyat-Allāh Āshtiyānī; Rafīʿī Qazwīnī; and the late Ruhollah Khomeini (d. 1989) in his well-known book, *Sharḥ Duʿā' Saḥar.*

One may claim that all these narratives and interpretations do not add to the credibility of the supplication's contents and that the chain ought to be authenticated. That will be discussed under the second method. This method, however, seems to indeed be realistic if combined with other methods, which should multiply the probability of its authentication and transmission.

The Second Method

Let us now deal with the second method, i.e. confirmation of narration by reliable narrators.

It is mentioned in the book of fasting and narrated by Ibn Abī Qurra with identical wordings as narrated from Ayyūb b. Yaqṭīn that he wrote to Abū l-Ḥasan, ʿAlī b. Mūsā al-Riḍā, asking him to approve this prayer. The Imam wrote back to him: "Yes, it is correct. Indeed it is my father's prayer, as he used to recite it during the nights of Ramaḍān. If people were aware of the greatness of these phrases before Almighty Allah and

[17] See *Tarājum al-rijāl,* by S. Aḥmad Ḥusaynī, v. 2, p. 757.

[18] See *Libāb al-alqāb fī alqāb al-aṭyāb,* p. 87.

[19] See *al-Dharīʿa ilā taṣānīf al-Shīʿa,* by Āqā Buzurg Tihrānī, v. 19, p. 9.

of how it enables them to receive a positive answer to their prayers, they would be willing to sacrifice their souls to memorise it, and Allah's mercy belongs solely to those who deserve it. And my father said: 'Imam al-Bāqir said: "If I swear by His holy name, I would not be consider it as lying that the great name (*al-ism al-aʿẓam*) of Almighty Allah is included within it! If you invoke Him, then you should do it praying wholeheartedly! It is indeed meant to remain secret, and knowledge of its secrets should not be disclosed to any except the privileged ones. The hypocrites, the liars, and the disbelievers must not be informed about it."'"

Muḥammad Bāqir al-Majlisī recalled (in *Biḥār al-anwār*): "We narrated it by ascribing it to my grandfather, Muḥammad b. al-Ḥasan al-Ṭūsī, Abū Jaʿfar al-Ṭūsī, on his support for ʿAlī b. al-Ḥasan b. Fadhdhāl from *The Book on Fasting*.

It is also narrated by Ibn Abī Qurra with identical wording, as they have both narrated that Ayyūb b. Yaqṭīn wrote to Abū l-Ḥasan ʿAlī b. Mūsā al-Riḍā asking him to explain the authenticity of this prayer. The Imam wrote to him: 'Yes, it is correct. Indeed it is my father's prayer, as he used to recite it during the nights of Ramaḍān. If people were aware of the greatness of these phrases before Almighty Allah and of how it enables them to receive a positive answer to their prayers, they would be willing to sacrifice their souls to memorise it, and Allah's mercy belongs solely to those who deserve it. And my father said: "Imam al-Bāqir said: 'If I swear by His holy name, I would not be considered as lying that the great name (*al-ism al-aʿẓam*) of Almighty Allah is included within it! If you invoke Him, then you should do it praying wholeheartedly! It is indeed meant to remain secret, and knowledge of its secrets should not be disclosed to any except the privileged ones. The hypocrites, the liars, and the disbelievers must not be informed about it.'"'"

One has now to elaborate on the chain of narrators. Shaykh al-Ṭūsī has narrated the supplication from ʿAlī b. al-Ḥasan b. Fadhdhāl in a chain to Muḥammad b. al-Zubayr. Most of the narrators in this chain are reliable (*thiqa*), but the only individual for whom there is no clear explicit statement about his reliability is Muḥammad b. al-Zubayr. He has been praised as a scholar, but has no explicit authentication. Some may be satisfied with the fact that he was a scholar and that Shaykh Ijāza issued the permission to narrate from him; others, however, may not consider that to be enough.

Therefore one may follow other paths, such as: 1) according to the late Muḥammad Bāqir al-Ṣadr (*naẓariyyat al-taʿwīḍ*), the theory of relying on extra chains that are narrated in other books but related to the same narrator, i.e. Aḥmad b. al-Ḥasan b. Fadhdhāl; or 2) basing its authenticity on a mathematic guess that when one analyses the same chain, which is narrated from al-Najāshī, one is led to certainty that it is the same chain, or that it is narrated at least two times through two chains, one by Shaykh al-Ṭūsī and one by Shaykh al-Najāshī. This evidence will lead one to the certainty of the perfection of its contents.[20]

The Third Method

A scholar was asked about the chain of narrators for this supplication, and he responded with a passage from Duʿā’ al-Ṣabāḥ of the Commander of the Faithful: "O He who guided to His essence with His essence and is transcendent beyond all likeness to His creatures!" Some might think that this response has nothing to do with the question, but in fact what the speaker intended to say was that the brilliance of the contents of Duʿā’ al-Saḥar is in itself the best evidence for its authenticity, such that it needs no chain of narrators. Its contents correspond to the verses of the Qur'an and other authentic supplications, such as Imam al-Ḥusayn's supplication on the Day of ʿArafa, Duʿā’ al-Ṣabāḥ, Duʿā’ Abū Ḥamza al-Thumālī, and Duʿā’ Jawshan al-Kabīr.

To illustrate this, let us take a verse of the Qur'an that corresponds to the teachings of this supplication: "God is the Light of the heavens and the earth. The parable of His light is a niche ..." (Q 25:35). The Qur'an uses the word "light" (*nūr*) to describe Allah as "the Light of the heavens

---

[20] See https://bit.ly/3QurawP, accessed on 25.07.2022.

and the earth."

In his commentary on this verse, Mullā Ṣadrā writes: "Sensible light is only called light because it is self-evident and needs nothing else to make it evident. On the contrary, it makes other things evident and brings them out of darkness."

Mullā Ṣadrā further writes: "The third aspect, which Sufis of recent times have mentioned, is in accordance with the 'possessors of unveilings (*mukāshifāt*)', 'the possessors of direct experience (*adhwāq*)', and the 'people of illuminations (*ishrāqāt*)'. It is based on the doctrines of the illuminationist philosophers and the ancient sages of Persia, which correspond to the traditions of the Prophet.

It is a narrative regarding the Prophet's Night Journey. He was questioned about his 'vision' to which he answered: 'It was a light that I saw,' meaning the Exalted is 'the light'. As it is impossible to connect the vision to Him, the Exalted, he assigned the word 'light' to Him, the Exalted." Then he goes on: "We have already delved into the position of [the illuminationist philosophers'] school of thought regarding light. In short, when the word is applied to sensible light (*al-nūr al-maḥsūs*) the light is manifest by itself and makes other things manifest. Its property is that it is sensible to the sense of sight and manifests objects of sight.

There is no problem in applying the word 'light' to it because sensible light is not the meaning of the word 'light' but an instance of it. If one were to find something else in this world that has the same property, the word would apply to it equally. It is akin to the meaning of scale (*mīzān*), which is 'something by which a thing is weighed' regardless of whether it has a lever and two pans or not – even though this is a common form of scale in this world ... According to this, applying 'light' to Him, the Exalted, would be based on the idea that it is the corroboration of its meaning and the subject of its name, because His essence is absolutely manifest by itself and manifests others. That is why the illuminationist philosophers technically apply 'Light of lights' to Him, the Exalted."

Then he goes on to state: "'Light', despite being something essential, is not other than the necessary essence of immaterial lights, both intellectual and spiritual [related to the psyche], except for the fact that it differs between them in terms of perfection and deficiency and there exists a hierarchy of greater and lesser intensity. Therefore it is applied to the essences of light by way of analogical gradation (*tashkīk*) because it cannot be proven logically that an essence can apply to many individuals by gradation. This is the reality of light: it has different levels of intensity, both strong and weak, and perfect and deficient. The apex of its perfection is the divine light (*al-nūr al-ilāhī*) – the Light Without Need (*al-nūr al-ghanī*) – beneath which lights are divided into intellectual and spiritual [related to the psyche] lights, while the next lower level of lights is divided into cosmic and terrestrial lights. In truth, the realities of 'light' and 'existence' are the same thing, and the existence of each thing is its manifestation ...

"In accordance with these definitions, the meaning of 'God is the Light of the heavens and the earth' would correspond to their saying 'Light of lights' or 'Existence of existences', for we have learned that the reality of everything is its existence, which is its luminosity. For example, Zayd, in reality, is a particular existence, and the light of his individual existence is evident in itself while making others evident ...

"Based on the last two aspects of these three interpretations, the word 'light' cannot be applied to the Necessary, the Exalted, merely as a metaphor or similitude, even though the theologians of Islam and a number of exegetes of the Qur'an have said that this phrase is meant to draw a similitude between the Real One and light, or that the meaning of light here is the Creator of light ...

"If one reflects deeply on the meaning of this derivative, they will arrive at the conclusion that the Exalted is, in reality, the Illuminator; in other words, He is the light in reality. Every agent in essence having the meaning of existential perfection must have within it that meaning of perfection, for the giver of perfection cannot be deficient in it, as intuition rules and demonstration agrees. If the meaning of light is found in Him, then either it is precisely the same as His essence or something additional to it ...

"The second would entail the dependency of the Exalted on a cause to emanate the meaning of light, because being attributed with something additional can only be through receptivity or deriving benefit from another, which is the opposite of originating something in another or providing benefits to another. If His essence is the illuminator of His essence, it necessitates His essence being receptive and active, in which case He would not be the simple reality. His simplicity, His oneness, and His sanctity from the blemishes of all compositions, however, have already been established; thus, this leads to a contradiction. Furthermore, it would entail His essence being more illuminating than Himself, which is impossible. If the principle of His luminosity is other than His essence, and other than His essence is one of the contingents, that would entail the dependence of the Necessary Being on the contingent for the attribution of perfection.

"If anyone denies the light to be perfection for being qua being, then let his mind be remedied if it has stopped [reflecting]. If he is arrogant, then Allah will sentence him to hell, where he will abide forever. However, he who contemplates on the knowledge that existence and light are united in meaning and reality but different in linguistic expression will no doubt hold that existence is perfection and good for every being qua being, and the Necessary is pure existence, so He is sheer light ...

"It has been investigated and established that light is the very reality of the Necessary Being Himself, may His glory be exalted. This is supported by the saying of the Commander of the Faithful and the Leader of the Monotheists: 'I would not worship a Lord I had not seen,' and it is strengthened by the saying of the Seal of the Prophets: 'There is no peace for the believers without meeting Allah.'"[21]

As such, this supplication contains lofty concepts about the unity and knowledge of Allah that corresponds to what can be understood from the verses of the Qur'an and the contents of other well-known

[21] Translation adapted from Mullā Ṣadrā, *On the Hermeneutics of the Light Verse of the Qurān*, trans. Peerwani, pp. 41-43.

supplications from the school of the Prophet's Ahl al-Bayt, such as those we have mentioned above. What is argued has been established, that Duʿāʾ al-Bahāʾ (al-Saḥar) was inspired to be transcribed (not authored) by one of Imam al-Riḍā's companions. Therefore, there is no reason to doubt the validity of its contents because its spiritual light is manifest for all those with sense or who give ear to it!

My efforts while applying the third method have most probably enabled us to achieve the goal of establishing that the content of this supplication is completely acceptable and in harmony with Shīʿī teachings endorsed by Muslim scholars. The reader can conclude from this article that this supplication contains interesting ideas, which one can counterfactually claim that had the eighth Imam, al-Riḍā, been present, he would have endorsed its reading by his followers. As such we do not need to insist that the author of the supplication was the Imam himself, as I have already established in the previous paragraphs. Indeed, all three methods were practically helpful, either separately or in combination, and lead us to increased confidence about the validity and authenticity of this supplication.

Conclusion

Duʿāʾ al-Bahāʾ (al-Saḥar) is the means by which a spiritual wayfarer journeys to Allah and in Allah while invoking the Lord of lords. It completes the supplicant's understanding of Allah as He has described Himself, not according to what the wayfarer's limited understanding comprehends. As such, one may conclude:

1. Duʿāʾ al-Bahāʾ (al-Saḥar) amongst the followers of the Ahl al-Bayt is a channel through which Muslims can become closer to the Almighty, while at the same time increase their knowledge and wisdom in recognising divinity.
2. Duʿāʾ al-Bahāʾ (al-Saḥar) is a perfect example of how to pray to the Almighty. To trace its chain of narrators (*sanad*), it was narrated by al-Majlisī in *Biḥār al-anwār*, and one may support

the reliability of its contents from the perspectives of theodicy, the technical rules within the science of narrations (*ʿilm al-ḥadīth*), and the contents of the Qur'an.

Bibliography

The Holy Qur'an.

S. Aḥmad Ḥusaynī, *Tarājum al-rijāl* (Majmaʿ al-Dhakhā'ir al-Islāmiyya: 1414/1993).

Ibn ʿArabī, *The Bezels of Wisdom*, trans. R. W. J. Austin (Paulist Press: 1980).

ʿAbd al-Razzāq Kāshānī, *Muʿjam iṣṭilāḥāt al-Ṣūfiyya* (Maktabat al-Ādāb: 2007).

Mullā Ḥabīb-Allāh Kāshānī, *Libāb al-alqāb fī alqāb al-aṭyāb* (Kitāb Furūshī-yi Bū Dharr-i Jumharī: 1958).

Muḥammad b. Isḥāq al-Qūnawī, *Risālat al-nuṣūṣ* (Āyat-i Ishrāq: 1390 Sh./2011).

Mīrzā Hāshim Ishkawarī, *Taʿlīqa bar Risālat al-nuṣūṣ-i Ṣadr al-Dīn-i Qūnawī*, ed. Jalāl al-Dīn Āshtiyānī (Markaz-i Nashr-i Dānishgāhī: 1983).

Mullā Ṣadrā, *On the Hermeneutics of the Light Verse of the Qurān*, trans. Peerwani (Islamic College for Advanced Studies Press: 2004).

Nahj al-balāgha, ed. Ṣubḥī al-Ṣāliḥ (Dār al-Kitāb al-Misrī: 2004).

Ibn Ṭāwūs, *Falāḥ al-sā'il* (al-Maktaba al-Ḥaydariyya: 2019).

Āqā Buzurg Tihrānī, *al-Dharīʿa ilā taṣānīf al-Shīʿa* (Ismāʿīliyān: 1408/1988).

Websites:

Stanford, "panentheism". Accessed 25 August 2022, https://plato.stanford.edu/entries/panentheism/

Ayatollah Maẓāhirī, *Sharḥ Duʿā' Saḥar*. Accessed 29 August 2023, https://shorturl.at/qHR04

Shaykh al-Ṭūsī, *Fihrist*. Accessed 25 July 2022, https://bit.ly/3QurawP

Shia Online Library, *Sharḥ Mullā Ṣāliḥ al-Māzandarānī*. Accessed 25 July 2022, https://bit.ly/3zppy0i

The Role of ʿ*Aql* in Qur'anic Exegesis: A Comparative Study of Traditional Shīʿī and Critical Rationalist Perspectives

Mohammed Ali Ismail[1]

The Islamic College

ABSTRACT

The role of *ʿaql* (reason or intellect) in Qur'anic exegesis (*tafsīr*) is subject to contrasting interpretations between traditional Shīʿī scholars of the Qur'an and critical rationalists. Traditional Shīʿī scholars of the Qur'an – i.e. those who adhere to a classical *uṣūlī* (rationalist) hermeneutical approach – regard *ʿaql* as a legitimate source of knowledge like the Qur'an and Sunna and assume it possesses religious authority (*ḥujjiyya sharʿiyya*). Within their framework, an exegetical method is the use of an authoritative source in exegesis, leading them to assert that reason-based exegesis (*tafsīr ʿaqlī*) is an important method in Qur'anic interpretation. In contrast, critical rationalists contend that traditional scholars have attributed an unwarranted role to *ʿaql* by equating it with a source of objective truths. According to critical rationalists, *ʿaql* encompasses two distinct cognitive faculties: *ʿaql* as "reason" distinguishes valid arguments from invalid ones, and *ʿaql* as "intellect" seeks to comprehend reality by developing, formulating, and assessing conjectures. *ʿAql* functions as a method solely in its capacity as reason, albeit with a function that diverges significantly from the traditional scholars' interpretation. This paper first introduces, compares, and contrasts the traditional Shīʿī and critical rationalist

[1] Director of Research and Publications and Senior Lecturer, The Islamic College, London, UK. Email: m.ismail@islamic-college.ac.uk

perspectives concerning the role of *ʿaql* in Qur'anic exegesis. It subsequently explores the implications of these differences on the typology and study of exegetical methods and approaches.

KEYWORDS: *ʿaql*, exegesis, traditional Shīʿī, critical rationalist, typology, exegetical methods, exegetical approaches

The perspective of traditional Shīʿī scholars on the role of *ʿaql* in Qur'anic exegesis

Generally, traditional Shīʿī scholars of the Qur'an[2] – i.e. those who adopt a classical *uṣūlī* hermeneutical approach to the study of Qur'anic exegesis[3] – hold the view that *ʿaql* is a valid source of knowledge like the Qur'an and Sunna. They consequently assume it possesses religious authority (*ḥujjiyya sharʿiyya*). One of the foundational pieces of evidence frequently cited by these scholars to substantiate their view is a hadith attributed to Imam Mūsā b. Jaʿfar al-Kāẓim. In this hadith, the Imam addresses his companion Hishām b. al-Ḥakam with the following words:

يَا هِشَامُ إِنَّ لِلّهِ عَلَى النَّاسِ حُجَّتَيْنِ حُجَّةً ظَاهِرَةً وَحُجَّةً بَاطِنَةً فَأَمَّا الظَّاهِرَةُ فَالرُّسُلُ وَالْأَنْبِيَاءُ وَالْأَئِمَّةُ وَأَمَّا الْبَاطِنَةُ فَالْعُقُولُ

O Hishām! God has two pieces of evidence for people: [one is] manifest, and [the other is] hidden. That which is manifest is His messengers, prophets, and Imams. That which is hidden is the

[2] My research specifically centres on the views of prominent traditional Shīʿī scholars of the Qur'an who have written on reason-based exegesis.

[3] *Uṣūlī* (rationalist) here is used in contrast to *akhbārī* (traditionist). *Uṣūlī*s are scholars of the Islamic discipline known as the Principles of Jurisprudence (*uṣūl al-fiqh*), which discusses Islamic legal theory and hermeneutics. For an overview of the *uṣūlī* and *akhbārī* positions, see Gleave (2013, pp. 26-29 and 184-186). For a detailed examination of the use of Shīʿī *uṣūlī* hermeneutics in Qur'anic exegesis, see Ṣādiqī (1391 (solar)/2012).

[people's] *'aql*.[4]

Traditional Shīʿī scholars argue that *'aql* being "evidence" means we must act according to its dictates. If it passes a definitive judgement on some issue, we must act according to it; otherwise, to regard it as evidence would be meaningless (Riḍāyī-Iṣfahānī 1390 (solar)/2011, p. 156).

Some traditional Shīʿī scholars further distinguish between various types of *'aql* and argue that it is the "demonstrative *'aql*" (*'aql-i burhānī*) that has this status, not the "lantern *'aql*" (*'aql-i miṣbāḥ*). In its capacity as the lantern *'aql*, *'aql* elucidates the meaning of Qur'anic verses by drawing upon other verses, hadiths, and resources such as lexicons. However, in its capacity as the demonstrative *'aql*, it is a source of knowledge, bestowing us with insights into various subjects. In the context of Qur'anic exegesis, it possesses an innate capacity to unveil the intended meanings of verses.

Ayatollah Jawādī-Āmulī, one of the most prominent Shīʿī exegetes today, explains the role of *'aql* in *tafsīr* as follows:

Reason-based exegesis (*tafsīr-i 'aqlī*), as mentioned previously, is done [in two ways:] either by making sense of internal and external evidence, in that an intelligent and sharp *'aql* understands the meaning of verses by putting verses and traditions together. In such a case, *'aql* only plays the role of a lantern, nothing more. As this type of rational endeavour-reason-based exegesis (*tafsīr-i ijtihādī-'aqlī*) is done by using transmitted sources, it [actually] comes under [the category of] "exegesis by reports" (*tafsīr bih ma'thūr*), not reason-based exegesis. Or, [reason-based exegesis is done] by inferring certain conceptual (*taṣawwurī*) and affirmational (*taṣdīqī*) principles from the inherent source of the demonstrative *'aql* and self-evident axioms. Here, *'aql* plays the role of a source (*manbaʿ*), not a mere lantern, [and this is what is really meant by reason-based exegesis] (1379 (solar)/2000, p. 170).

At this juncture, it is noteworthy that traditional Shīʿī scholars employ

---

[4] Al-Kulaynī, 1429 (lunar)/2008, v. 1, p. 35.

various terminologies to describe reason-based exegesis.[5] For example, Ayatollah Muḥammad Hādī Maʿrifat (1418 (lunar)/1997, p. 349) and Muḥammad ʿAlī Ayāzī (1414 (lunar)/1993), p. 40) refer to it as "rational endeavour exegesis" (*tafsīr-i ijtihādī*); ʿAlī al-Ālūsī (1370 (solar)/1991, p. 246) uses the term "rational endeavour-reason-based exegesis" (*tafsīr ijtihādī-ʿaqlī*); and, as previously mentioned, Ayatollah Jawādī-Āmulī applies the term "rational endeavour-reason-based exegesis" when *ʿaql* functions as a lantern. These examples illustrate that while there are some similarities in the terminology used by these authors for reason-based exegesis, there is no uniformity. The same variability applies to their definitions of this type of exegesis; while common elements exist, there is no consensus on its precise scope and boundaries.

In his definition of reason-based exegesis, ʿAlawī-Mihr, another contemporary Shīʿī scholar in the field of Qur'anic studies, draws extensively from the writings of Ayatollah Jawādī-Āmulī:

It is [a type of] exegesis that discovers religious rulings and the teachings and truths of verses of the Qur'an by using the demonstrative *ʿaql* and rational indicators (*qarā'in-i ʿaqlī*) as a source rather than merely as a lantern or tool (1394 (solar)/2015, p. 252).

ʿAlawī-Mihr concludes that reason-based exegesis can be categorised into two distinct types:

1. Specific (*khāṣṣ*): this type of exegesis relies on the demonstrative *ʿaql* and represents exegesis in its truest form.
2. General (*ʿāmm*): this type of exegesis is conducted through the lantern *ʿaql* (p. 262).

Another prominent traditional Shīʿī scholar, Ayatollah Makārim-Shīrāzī, highlights the significance of the demonstrative *ʿaql* in his explanation of reason-based exegesis:

---

[5] Some notable works widely regarded as reason-based exegesis are *al-Tibyān fī tafsīr al-Qur'ān* by Muḥammad b. al-Ḥasan al-Ṭūsī (d. 1067), *Majmaʿ al-bayān* by Faḍl b. Ḥasan al-Ṭabrisī (d. 1153), *Mafātīḥ al-ghayb* (*al-Tafsīr al-kabīr*) by Fakhr al-Dīn al-Rāzī (d. 1209), *Rūḥ al-maʿānī* by Maḥmūd al-Ālūsī (d. 1853), and *Tafsīr al-mīzān* by Muḥammad Ḥusayn Ṭabāṭabā'ī (d. 1981).

The meaning of exegesis by *ʿaql* is that we seek the support of evident rational indicators, which are acceptable to all rational minds, in understanding the meaning of words and sentences in texts like the Qur'an and Hadith. For example, when it is stated: "The hand of God is over their hands,"[6] *ʿaql* says certainly "the hand of God" does not refer to the particular limb that has five fingers because God definitely does not have a body as every body is limited and destined to perish, and God is not limited nor destined to perish; He is pre-eternal (*azalī*) and post-eternal (*abadī*). Instead, what is meant is the "power of God", which is above the power of all others. The hand is used metaphorically to mean power because the hand manifests an individual's power in action.

Wherever there is mention of exegesis by *ʿaql*, what is meant is this sort of exegesis, not the imposition [of one's opinions], personal preferences, poor arguments, and baseless opinions (1378 (solar)/1988, pp. 38-39).

This examination of the traditional Shīʿī perspective will conclude by delving into the viewpoint of the contemporary scholar of the Qur'an, Riḍāyī-Iṣfahānī. His book, *Rawish-hā wa girāyish-hā-yi tafsīrī-yi Qur'ān* (1390 (solar)/2011), which constitutes volume two of his five-volume series titled *Mantiq-i tafsīr-i Qur'ān*, is widely regarded as one of the foremost textbooks on this subject within Shīʿī seminaries and undergraduate programmes.[7] After comparing and critically evaluating the views of various Muslim authors, Riḍāyī-Iṣfahānī concludes that the method of reason-based exegesis encompasses the following dual dimensions:

One: the use of demonstrative proof (*burhān*) and rational indicators (*qarā'in-i ʿaqlī*) in exegesis as a means to clarify the concepts and intent of Qur'anic verses. Here, *ʿaql* is a source and tool for the exegesis of the Qur'an, and rational judgements and demonstrative proofs become

---

[6] Q 48:10.

[7] This work has been translated into English as *A Textbook on the Methods of Qur'anic Exegesis* (2018, ICAS Press). It is a core reading book on the Approaches to Exegesis module that I teach at The Islamic College, London.

indicators for the exegesis of verses. This type of *ʿaql* is variously called the "acquired *ʿaql*", "decisive rational judgements", and the "demonstrative *ʿaql*".

Two: the use of the faculty of thinking to gather verses (while considering traditions, lexicons etc.) and making inferences from them to clarify the concepts and intent of verses. The product of this endeavour is "rational endeavour exegesis" (*tafsīr-i ijtihādī*) of the Qur'an. In this case, *ʿaql* is a lantern and discoverer. This type of intellect is called "the inherent *ʿaql*", "the faculty of thinking", and "the faculty of perception" (pp. 154-155).

Riḍāyī-Iṣfahānī proceeds to explain that, according to the majority view, both types of reason-based exegesis are regarded as constituting the method. Nevertheless, he posits that "what is stated in the second definition is known as reason-based exegesis with a degree of inaccuracy, and in truth, reason-based exegesis is what is stated in the first definition" (p. 155).

Riḍāyī-Iṣfahānī's perspective on the role of *ʿaql* in Qur'anic exegesis can be summarised as follows:

1. *ʿAql* is a knowledge source. It is a knowledge source because it is authoritative evidence (*ḥujja*), as is the Qur'an and Sunna. *ʿAql* being an authority means we must base our actions on definitive judgements made by it.
2. We have proof that *ʿaql* is an authority, such as the hadith attributed to Imam Mūsā b. Jaʿfar al-Kāẓim, previously cited.
3. Although *ʿaql* is a knowledge source, it is not at the same level as the other two knowledge sources (Qur'an and Sunna). Instead, the position of *ʿaql* as a source of knowledge is below that of the Qur'an and Sunna. *ʿAql* makes discoveries from the Qur'an and Sunna; hence, human beings will always need divine revelation (pp. 154-156).
4. As *ʿaql* is a knowledge source, and a knowledge source is a "method" (Arabic: *manhaj*; Persian: *rawish*) in Qur'anic exegesis

(p. 22), it logically follows that *ʿaql* is a method for interpreting the Qur'an. This principle also applies to the Qur'an and Sunna, both of which are knowledge sources and, consequently, exegetical methods.

An example of the traditional approach

The traditional perspective asserts that reason-based exegesis can be traced back to the time of the Infallibles. According to this viewpoint, the following report illustrates an instance of an Imam engaging in reason-based exegesis when addressing a question about the interpretation of a Qur'anic verse:

كُنْتُ فِي مَجْلِسِ أَبِي جَعْفَرٍ عَلَيْهِ السَّلَامُ إِذْ دَخَلَ عَلَيْهِ عَمْرُو بْنُ عُبَيْدٍ فَقَالَ لَهُ جُعِلْتُ فِدَاكَ قَوْلُ اللهِ تَبَارَكَ وَتَعَالىٰ ﴿وَمَنْ يَحْلِلْ عَلَيْهِ غَضَبِي فَقَدْ هَوىٰ﴾ مَا ذٰلِكَ الْغَضَبُ فَقَالَ أَبُو جَعْفَرٍ عَلَيْهِ السَّلَامُ هُوَ الْعِقَابُ يَا عَمْرُو إِنَّهُ مَنْ زَعَمَ أَنَّ اللّٰهَ قَدْ زَالَ مِنْ شَيْءٍ إِلىٰ شَيْءٍ فَقَدْ وَصَفَهُ صِفَةَ مَخْلُوقٍ وَإِنَّ اللهَ تَعَالىٰ لَايَسْتَفِزُّهُ شَيْءٌ فَيُغَيِّرَهُ

I was in Abū Jaʿfar [al-Bāqir]'s session when ʿAmr b. ʿUbayd suddenly entered. ʿAmr asked him: "May I be your ransom! In the statement of God, the Blessed and Exalted, 'He upon whom My wrath descends will definitely perish,'[8] what is this wrath?" Abū Jaʿfar [al-Bāqir] said: "It is punishment, O ʿAmr! One who thinks God has changed from one state to another has thereby described Him as one describes a creature. Indeed, nothing provokes God thereby changing Him."[9]

This interpretation exemplifies reason-based exegesis, unfolding through the following logical progression: when humans become angry, they undergo a change in their emotional state. However, God is immutable, remaining constant and unchanging. Therefore, a literal

[8] Q 20:81.

[9] Al-Kulaynī 1429 (lunar)/2008, v. 1, pp. 270-271.

reading of the verse would be incorrect as it would ascribe human-like anger to God. Instead, the verse is to be understood metaphorically to mean that God will punish the person with whom He is displeased.

The perspective of critical rationalists on the role of *ʿaql* in Qur'anic exegesis

Critical rationalism is a school of thought developed during the mid-twentieth century by the Austrian-British philosopher Karl Popper (d. 1996).[10] One of Popper's most famous quotations captures the essence of the critical rationalist philosophical outlook (1994, p. xii):

It is a way of thinking, and even a way of living: a readiness to listen to critical arguments, to search for one's own mistakes, and to learn from them. It is, fundamentally, an attitude that I have tried to formulate (perhaps first in 1932) in the following two lines:

"I may be wrong and you may be right,
and by an effort, we may get nearer to the truth."

These lines reflect the core principles of critical rationalism, emphasising the importance of open-mindedness, self-critique, and the ongoing pursuit of truth through critical inquiry and learning from one's mistakes.

Critical rationalists present a notably different perspective on the nature and role of *ʿaql* compared to traditional Shīʿī scholars. According to Paya, a prominent Muslim critical rationalist, *ʿaql* encompasses two distinct cognitive faculties, expressed in English as "reason" and "intellect". In its function as reason, *ʿaql* distinguishes valid arguments from invalid ones, while in its function as intellect, it seeks to comprehend reality by developing, formulating, and assessing conjectures (Paya 2022, pp. 45-46).

According to critical rationalists, reason serves as a tool for

---

[10] For a short account of his life, see Popper, *The Philosophy of Karl Popper*, ed. Paul Arthur Schilpp (1974), and Miller, *Out of Error* (2006). For a sample of Popper's works, see Popper, *Popper Selections*, ed. David Miller (1985).

assessing the logical coherence of the form and structure, as opposed to the content, of arguments. On the other hand, the intellect's role is to formulate conjectures and apply them to reality. The content of knowledge claims cannot be assessed by any inherent truths stored in *ʿaql* as posited by traditional Shīʿī scholars. This is because *ʿaql* does not inherently contain actual knowledge claims. Instead, the content of conjectures undergoes assessment in two ways: firstly, conjectures that have empirical content or deal with empirically accessible aspects of reality are assessed through empirical testing and analytical (i.e. rational, logical, and philosophical) processes. Secondly, conjectures lacking empirically testable content or pertaining to aspects of reality beyond empirical accessibility, such as assertions about the existence of angels, are assessed through analytical means. Additionally, these claims can be indirectly assessed by considering the empirical or practical implications that may arise from them.

Critical rationalists maintain that, unlike the Qur'an and Sunna, *ʿaql,* in its function as reason, makes no knowledge claims and cannot be deemed a knowledge source since knowledge sources serve as repositories of knowledge claims. *ʿAql,* in its role as intellect, does make knowledge claims, but it does so by formulating conjectures; *formulating* conjectural knowledge claims is different from being a *source* of knowledge. Whereas the knowledge claims made by the Qur'an and authentic Sunna are true and infallible, those made by our intellect are fallible. We can better understand the content of the Qur'an and Sunna by successively correcting the defects of our proposed conjectures. Within the realm of *tafsīr,* these conjectures are expressed as interpretations of the Qur'anic text.

As for the hadiths about *ʿaql* being *ḥujja*, critical rationalists provide an interpretation that significantly diverges from traditional Shīʿī scholars. According to critical rationalists, the Qur'an, prophets, and Imams hold the status of *ḥujja* as authorities, providing valuable information that can be relied upon and tested against our conjectural understanding of their wisdom. However, *ʿaql* serves as *ḥujja* in a different sense: in its role as reason, it functions as a tool which authoritatively enables us to assess the form of knowledge claims. While the Qur'an, prophets, and Imams guide us by offering reliable information and correcting our erroneous conjectures, *ʿaql* guides us by assessing the correctness of our arguments by examining their logical and rational validity.

The diagram below illustrates the critical rationalist perspective on the development of conjectures from the point of their emergence through to becoming objective knowledge. Every conjecture, produced in response to a genuine problem presented by reality to the inquirer, begins as a lived experience, intuition, or flash of insight. Next, the intellect transforms these into thoughts by utilising memory, concepts, and language; this is the first stage of the individual's "understanding". Then, the intellect employs reason to translate these thoughts into publicly accessible and assessable arguments; this is "explanation" (Paya 2022, p. 83).

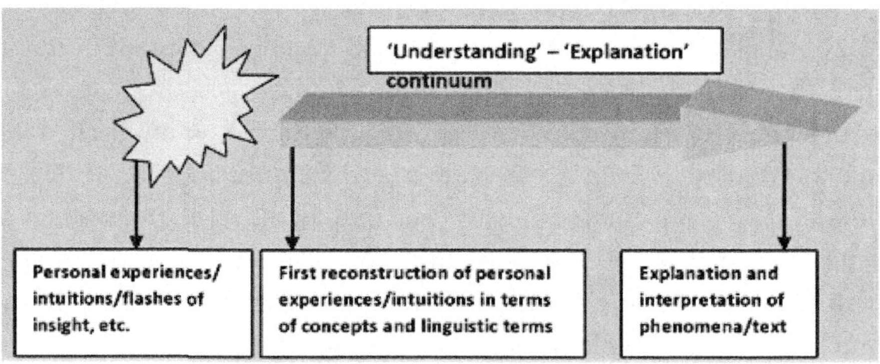

Understanding-Explanation Continuum
(Diagram courtesy of ICAS Press)

Critical rationalists argue that the growth of knowledge hinges on the elimination of errors in our proposed conjectural solutions. As the final arbiter, reality either corroborates or refutes our conjectures, thereby enhancing our understanding of it. In essence, our acquisition of knowledge about reality occurs through two avenues: *via positiva* and *via negativa*. Knowledge *via positiva* is the sum of all our conjectures, which, so far and despite our best efforts to expose their shortcomings, have remained unrefuted. Knowledge *via negativa* is the sum of all our conjectures which have been shown to be false, indicating that the reality in question does not align with those conjectures. The process of refining our understanding through interaction with reality is never-ending, as we can never obtain the complete and absolute truth about any facet of reality. Even if, by chance, we were to stumble upon such truth, we would not be able to conclusively ascertain its status as such because of our limited cognitive abilities on the one hand and the indefinite richness and complexity of reality on the other (Popper 1979 and 1994).

An example of the critical rationalist approach

Paya (2018, pp. 38-39) offers an example from the Qur'an that he contends corroborates and endorses the critical rationalist approach to knowledge development. This example is found in Q 6:76-79, where Prophet Abraham delivers a compelling demonstration to the polytheists.

فَلَمَّا جَنَّ عَلَيْهِ ٱلَّيْلُ رَءَا كَوْكَبًا قَالَ هَٰذَا رَبِّى فَلَمَّآ أَفَلَ قَالَ لَآ أُحِبُّ ٱلْءَافِلِينَ

When the night grew dark over him, he saw a star and said: "This is my Lord," but when it set, he said: "I do not like things that set."

فَلَمَّا رَءَا ٱلْقَمَرَ بَازِغًا قَالَ هَٰذَا رَبِّى فَلَمَّآ أَفَلَ قَالَ لَئِن لَّمْ يَهْدِنِى رَبِّى لَأَكُونَنَّ مِنَ ٱلْقَوْمِ ٱلضَّآلِّينَ

And when he saw the moon rising, he said: "This is my Lord," but when it too set, he said: "If my Lord does not guide me, I shall be one of those who go astray."

فَلَمَّا رَءَا ٱلشَّمْسَ بَازِغَةً قَالَ هَٰذَا رَبِّى هَٰذَآ أَكْبَرُ فَلَمَّآ أَفَلَتْ قَالَ يَٰقَوْمِ إِنِّى بَرِىٓءٌ مِّمَّا تُشْرِكُونَ

Then he saw the sun rising and cried: "This is my Lord! This is greater." But when the sun set, he said: "My people, I disown all that you worship beside God.

إِنِّى وَجَّهْتُ وَجْهِىَ لِلَّذِى فَطَرَ ٱلسَّمَٰوَٰتِ وَٱلْأَرْضَ حَنِيفًا وَمَآ أَنَا۠ مِنَ ٱلْمُشْرِكِينَ

I have turned my face as a true believer towards Him who created the heavens and the earth. I am not one of the polytheists."

In his demonstration, Prophet Abraham employs a series of conjectures, each suggesting that a celestial body might be God. When reality exposes the shortcomings of a conjecture, he replaces it with a better one. Each time he does this, there is a growth of knowledge for the people *via negativa* as they learn what cannot be God. The conclusion is that God, as the unchanging source of guidance, help, and benefit, cannot be associated with entities that disappear.

After examining both the traditional and critical rationalist viewpoints, it becomes apparent that although both groups of scholars agree that *ʿaql* is a tool and method for interpreting the Qur'an, they differ considerably in their reasons for why *ʿaql* serves as an exegetical method and the role it plays. Traditional Shīʿī scholars view *ʿaql* as an exegetical method because it is a knowledge source, whereas critical rationalists consider *ʿaql*, in its function as reason, an exegetical method because it evaluates the form of arguments. The implications of these differences on the typology and study of exegetical methods and approaches will now be explored.

Implications of the two perspectives on the typology and study of exegetical methods and approaches

Typologies of exegetical methods and approaches and their importance

Typologies of exegetical methods and approaches help us determine the particular genre to which a *tafsīr* can be attributed, and they make it easier to compare and contrast various exegeses. Moreover, the process of classification necessitates thoughtful judgement, requiring us to critically evaluate why certain labels are apt for categorising these works. For instance, when examining Ṭabāṭabā'ī's *al-Mīzān*, certain questions arise: should it be classified as a philosophical exegetical work due to its use of philosophical *methods*? Or is it more accurate to consider *al-Mīzān* as adopting a philosophical *approach* among various other approaches? This evaluative dimension of classification aids us in scrutinising exegetical works, prompting us to explore in greater depth the hermeneutical frameworks and tools employed by their authors.

Through my experience of teaching courses on methods and approaches of Qur'anic exegesis to undergraduate and graduate students, it has become evident that the categorisation of exegetical methods and approaches plays a crucial role in shaping our understanding of them. In Islamic studies, courses and texts on Qur'anic hermeneutical methods and approaches tend to be structured around a specific typology. The selection of methods and approaches for discussion and how they are perceived is heavily influenced by the typology adopted by the course or text.

Typologies of Qur'anic exegesis

Ignác Goldziher is credited with being the first person to have written specifically on Qur'anic exegetical methods and approaches. His *Richtungen der Islamischen Koranauslegung* was first published in 1920 and has since been translated into Arabic in 1944 and 1955, Persian in 2004, and English in 2006 (Zadeh 2015, p. 329). Goldziher divided Qur'anic exegetical works into the early stages, traditional exegesis (Sunnī works with a linguistic or hadith-based approach), dogmatic exegesis (focused on theological disputes), mystical exegesis, sectarian exegesis, and modern exegesis.

Among the notable works originally authored in English on this subject is John Wansbrough's 1977 book, *Quranic Studies: Sources and Methods of Scriptural Interpretation.* Wansbrough borrowed terminology from the Jewish exegetical tradition to classify early exegetical texts into haggadic (narrative), halakhic (legal), masoretic (textual), rhetorical, and allegorical types. Johanna Pink's research in 2010 is also noteworthy for her development of a typology for modern *tafsīr* by analysing modern Arabic, Turkish, Malay, and Indonesian *tafsīr* works (2010a and 2010b).

The first book originally written in Arabic that systematically classified works of exegesis was Muḥammad Ḥusayn al-Dhahabī's *al-Tafsīr wa-l-mufassirūn* (Exegesis and Exegetes), first published in 1961. In response to al-Dhahabī's treatment of Shīʿī exegesis and aiming to present a more accurate representation of exegetical works and their authors, Ayatollah Muḥammad Hādī Maʿrifat wrote *al-Tafsīr wa-l-mufassirūn fī thawbihi al-qashīb* (Exegesis and Exegetes in New Clothes) in 1409 (lunar)/1988.

In recent decades, a substantial body of Persian literature has enriched this field. Notable publications include ʿAbbās ʿAlī ʿUmayd Zanjānī's *Mabānī wa rawish-hā-yi tafsīrī-yi Qur'ān* (Foundations and Exegetical Methods of the Qur'an) in 1366 (solar)/1987; Sayyid Riḍā Mu'addab's *Rawish-hā-yi tafsīr-i Qur'ān* (Methods of Exegesis of the Qur'an) in 1380 (solar)/2001; Ḥusayn ʿAlawī-Mihr's *Rawish-hā wa girāyish-hā-yi tafsīrī* (Exegetical Methods and Orientations) in 1381 (solar)/2002; ʿAlī Akbar Bābā'ī's *Makātib-i tafsīrī* (Exegetical Schools) in 1381 solar/2002; Muḥammad ʿAlī Riḍāyī-Iṣfahānī's *Rawish-hā wa girāyish-hā-yi tafsīrī-yi Qur'ān* (Exegetical Methods and Orientations of the Qur'an) in 1390 (solar)/2011, which is the second volume of his five-volume series, *Manṭiq-i tafsīr-i Qur'ān* (Logic of Exegesis of the Qur'an); and the encyclopaedia entry in volume seven of *Dānishnāmih-yi jihān-i Islām* (1383 (solar)/2004), which has been translated into English as *Tafsir: Qur'anic Exegesis: An Entry from Encyclopaedia of the World of Islam* (2012). The authors of these works utilise various approaches to categorise exegetical works and employ a wide array of terms to label the categories, such as exegetical "foundations", "methods", "methodologies", "schools", "orientations", and "approaches".

A traditional Shīʿī typology

In his highly popular textbook mentioned earlier, Riḍāyī-Iṣfahānī (1390 (solar)/2011) distinguishes between exegetical "methods" and "approaches":

Methods [are] the use of specific tools or sources in Qur'an interpretation to clarify the meaning and intent of its verses and arrive at distinct conclusions. In other words, how an exegete discovers and extracts the meanings and intent from the verses (p. 22).

Approaches [are] the influence of religious and doctrinal beliefs and trends in the exegete's era, and the exegete's style of *tafsīr*, which is shaped by his beliefs, objectives, tastes, preferences, and academic specialisation (p. 23).

In an interview I conducted with Riḍāyī-Iṣfahānī, he emphasised that in the realm of Qur'anic exegesis, it is the knowledge source that distinguishes an exegetical method from an exegetical approach. He explained that the term "method" is a homonym and carries a particular meaning in Qur'anic exegesis. Just as the word "Shaykh" refers to "Ibn Sīnā" (Avicenna) in philosophy but to "Ṭūsī" (Muḥammad b. Ḥasan al-Ṭūsī) in jurisprudence, the term "method" takes on various meanings within different contexts. In the context of Qur'anic exegesis, "method" assumes a specific definition provided by experts in the field.

I also interviewed ʿAlawī-Mihr, whose work I referenced earlier. He explained that knowledge sources are considered methods because the religion regards them as credible and authoritative (*ḥujja*). The religious authority (*ḥujjiyyat-i sharʿī*) of a knowledge source makes it a method; therefore, since the Qur'an, Sunna, and *ʿaql* are all authoritative, they are methods. When these authoritative sources of knowledge are employed for exegetical purposes, they function as methods of *tafsīr*. ʿAlawī-Mihr defined method as "the use of a knowledge source that has religious authority." He referred to the view of Ayatollah Jawādī-Āmulī, who contends that if something in science is certain, it is authoritative. Therefore, "scientific" (*ʿilmī*) exegesis is considered a knowledge source and a method based on the premise that it uses accurate and authoritative scientific knowledge in exegesis.

The diagram below illustrates Riḍāyī-Iṣfahānī's typology of exegetical methods and approaches.[11] As can be seen, the reason-based method is placed alongside the intratextual exegetical method (*tafsīr al-Qurʾān bil-Qurʾān*),[12] the tradition-based exegetical method (*tafsīr bil-riwāya*),[13] the scientific (*ʿilmī*) method,[14] the allegorical (*ishārī*) method,[15] and the amalgamate (*jāmiʿ*) method.[16]

[11] The aim of this section, along with the following sections, is to compare and contrast a traditional Shīʿī typology with a critical rationalist one to understand how these different paradigms influence their typologies, and how these typologies, in turn, impact the study of exegetical methods and approaches. Riḍāyī-Iṣfahānī's typology was chosen due to the widespread use of his work as a primary textbook in Shīʿī seminaries and undergraduate programmes.

[12] In this method, verses of the Qur'an are used to interpret other verses.

[13] This method involves using reports of the Sunna, which incorporates the words, actions, and tacit approvals of Prophet Muḥammad, his daughter Fāṭima al-Zahrāʾ, and the Twelve Imams, to interpret verses of the Qur'an.

[14] This method employs empirical science to gain a better understanding of verses with scientific content.

[15] In this method, the exegete delves beyond the apparent meaning of the verses to explain their hidden aspects and inner meanings.

[16] Also called "the meta-method", this is a comprehensive method that acts like an umbrella under which several methods can be used.

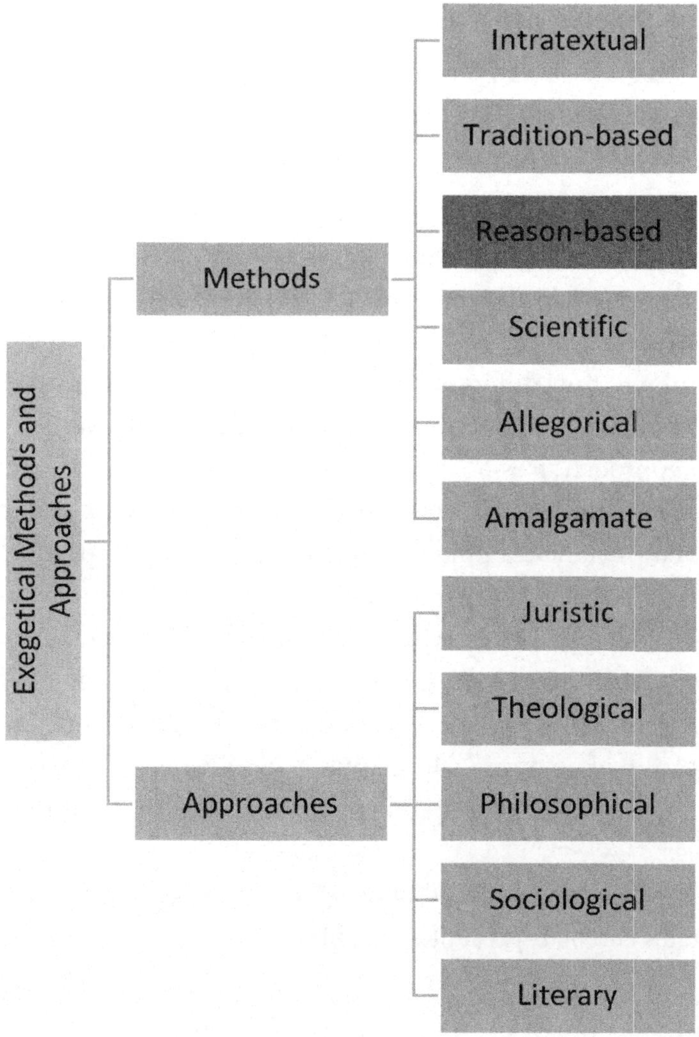

A critical rationalist perspective

From a critical rationalist perspective, "Methods are 'tools'. They are used in various sciences and disciplines to either facilitate the task of exploring or investigating different aspects of reality (whether natural or socially constructed) by assisting researchers/practitioners to collect data or help them to achieve specific practical goals through taking certain concrete steps" (Paya 2022, p. 10). Methods are technologies, serving two primary purposes:

1. fulfilling our non-cognitive needs; and
2. acting as tools to facilitate our cognitive pursuits. As such, they are not knowledge themselves but tools for obtaining data and assessing conjectures/interpretations.[17]

Methods vary according to the approach taken by an exegete. An "approach" in this context is the perspective and theoretical framework that the exegete adopts when considering the verses. An approach can be likened to a lens through which the exegete examines the Qur'anic text. Similar to how different lenses alter one's perception, an exegete's chosen approach influences how they interpret the Qur'an.

Each approach uses a constellation of methods and brings its own terminology, concepts, principles, fundamental assumptions, and axioms. For instance, a philosophical approach to interpreting a verse may employ "the causality principle".[18] Certain methods may be shared across several approaches, whereas others might be specific to a single approach. Furthermore, an exegete may employ multiple approaches when interpreting Qur'anic verses, as seen in Ṭabāṭabāʾī's *al-Mīzān*. The selection of an approach or approaches by an exegete depends on various factors, including their academic specialisation, interests, and objectives.

Based on what was stated above, Qur'anic exegetical methods and approaches can be represented as follows:

---

[17] Traditional Shīʿī scholars often employ the term "*qawāʾid*" (principles) to denote what critical rationalists call "methods". This usage can be observed in works such as al-Maybudī's *al-Qawāʾid al-tafsīr ladā l-Shīʿa wa-l-Sunna* (Principles of Exegesis According to the Shīʿa and Ahl al-Sunna) (2007), Riḍāyī-Iṣfahānī's *Manṭiq-i tafsīr-i Qurʾān (1): mabānī wa qawāʾid-i tafsīr-i Qurʾān* (Logic of Exegesis of the Qur'an (1): Foundations and Principles of the Exegesis of the Qur'an) (1387 (solar)/2008), and ʿAlī Akbar Bābāʾī's *Qawāʾid-i tafsīr-i Qurʾān* (Principles of the Exegesis of the Qur'an) (1394 (solar)/2015).

[18] See, for example, Ṭabāṭabāʾī's exegesis of Sūrat al-Fātiḥa (Q 1:1) (1390 (lunar)/1970, v. 1, p. 24).

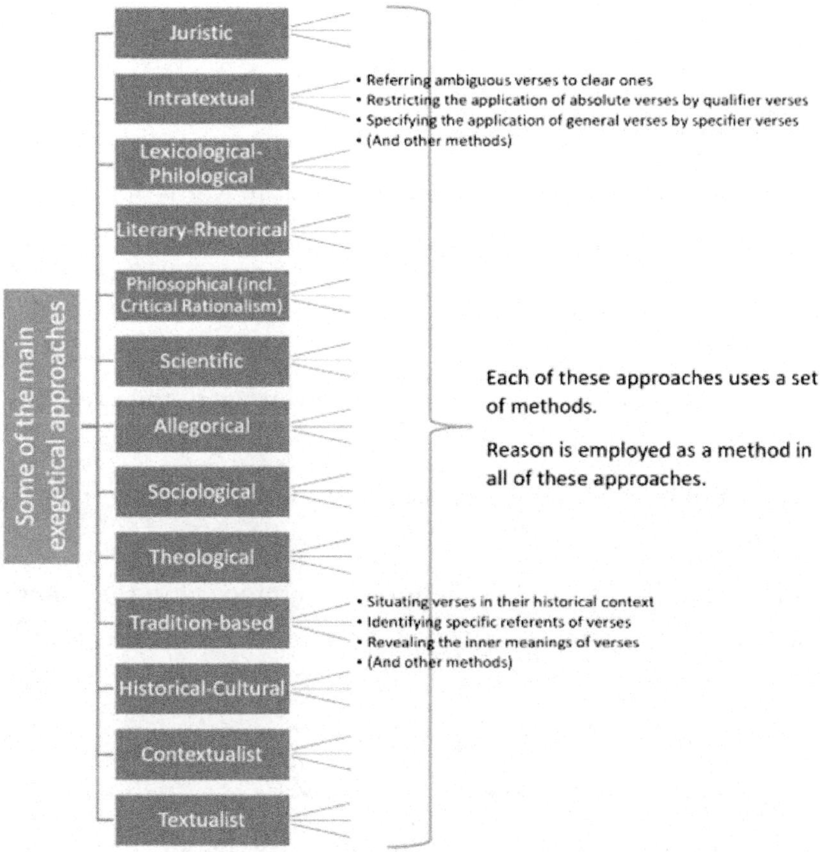

As an example, methods used in the intratextual approach include the following (due to space limitations, only the first three are shown on the diagram):

1. Referring the ambiguous (*mutashābih*) verses to clear (*muḥkam*) ones.
2. Restricting the application of absolute (*muṭlaq*) verses by qualifier (*muqayyid*) verses.
3. Specifying the application of general (*ʿāmm*) verses by specifier (*mukhāṣṣiṣ*) verses.
4. Interpreting ambiguous (*mujmal*) verses by clarifier (*mubayyin*)

verses.

5. Determining the referent (*miṣdāq*) of a verse by examining other verses.
6. Using the literary context (*siyāq*) of a verse.
7. Collating similar verses (similar, that is, in words or content).
8. Resolving apparent contradictions between verses.
9. Determining the meaning of Qur'anic terms with the assistance of other verses.
10. Giving preference to a meaning of a verse with the assistance of other verses.
11. Combining the abrogating (*nāsikh*) and abrogated (*mansūkh*) verses.[19]

Another example pertains to the methods employed in the tradition-based approach (again, only the first three are shown on the diagram):

1. Situating verses in their historical context.
2. Identifying the referent of verses.
3. Revealing the inner meanings of verses.
4. Clarifying the meaning of words and sentences.
5. Providing detail, particularly to laws, eschatological matters, and stories.
6. Specifying the application of general verses.
7. Restricting the application of absolute verses.
8. Identifying abrogating and abrogated verses.

Exegetical approaches can be further divided into sub-categories or types, each with its own set of methods. For instance, within the

[19] Riḍāyī-Iṣfahānī 1390 (solar)/2011, pp. 72-82. The author describes them as "sub-types" of the intratextual method rather than methods used by the intratextual approach.

philosophical approach, critical rationalism can be identified as a sub-category, employing the "conjectures and refutations" method. Likewise, the theological approach can be sub-divided into Ashʿarī, Muʿtazilī, Māturīdī, and Twelver Shīʿī categories. Similarly, the juristic approach can be sub-divided into Ḥanafī, Ḥanbalī, Mālikī, Shāfiʿī, and Jaʿfarī categories, as illustrated below. While some methods may be shared among these sub-categories, others might be particular to one sub-category.

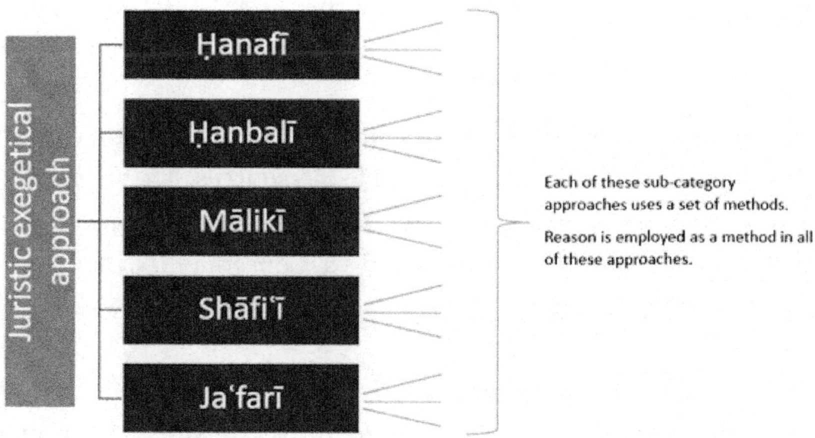

This alternative to the traditional typology is uncomplicated and precise, making it easy to understand while accurately representing the main exegetical methods and approaches used to interpret the Qur'an. It notably integrates reason-based exegesis as a method across all approaches rather than placing it as a separate category. Furthermore, while the illustrated typology is not meant to be exhaustive, it includes several important approaches that are not mentioned in the traditional classification.

Conclusion

Traditional Shīʿī scholars and critical rationalists approach their analysis of *ʿaql* from different paradigms, resulting in divergent views on its function and role in Qur'anic exegesis. While both recognise reason-based exegesis as a method in *tafsīr*, their definitions of what constitutes a method vary considerably. Thus, when reading the works of traditional scholars and critical rationalists on Qur'an interpretation, it becomes paramount to grasp the nuanced meanings they attribute to the terms they use.

Beyond terminology variations, such as "demonstrative *ʿaql*" and "lantern *ʿaql*" versus "reason" and "intellect", and different interpretations of shared terms like "method" and "approach", lie fundamental disparities in epistemological principles that underpin their viewpoints.

Prominent traditional Shīʿī scholars contend that exegetical methods serve as authoritative knowledge sources. They view *ʿaql* as an authoritative source of knowledge, much like the Qur'an and Sunna, unveiling the meaning of the Qur'anic text. Consequently, they consider *tafsīr ʿaqlī* an important hermeneutical method for comprehending the Qur'an.

In contrast, critical rationalists regard methods as tools that serve non-cognitive needs and facilitate cognitive pursuits. According to their perspective, *ʿaql* does not function as a source of knowledge; instead, it qualifies as a method in Qur'anic exegesis because, in its function as reason, it assesses the logical validity of our conjectures. Within the context of Qur'anic exegesis, these conjectures assume the role of interpretations.

The disparities between the two perspectives have significant implications for students studying exegetical methods and approaches and for educators teaching the subject. While critical rationalist scholars in Qur'anic studies remain relatively few in number, growing academic interest in critical rationalism within certain segments of Islamic studies suggests that the implications of this trend may become more substantial in the future.

Bibliography

Adel, G.H., Elmi, M.J., and Taromi-Rad, H. (eds.), *Tafsir: Qur'anic Exegesis. An Entry from Encyclopaedia of the World of Islam* (London: EWI Press: 2012).

ʿĀdil, G.Ḥ. (ed.), *Dānishnāmih-yi jihān-i Islām* (Tehran: Bunyād-i Dā'irat al-Maʿārif-i Islāmī: 1383 (solar)/2004).

ʿAlawī-Mihr, Ḥ., *Rawish-hā wa girāyish-hā-yi tafsīrī* (Qum: Intishārāt-i Uswa: 1381 (solar)/2002).

_____ "Jaryānshināsī-yi tafāsīr-i ʿaqlī-yi muʿāṣir," in *Jaryānshināsī-yi tafāsīr dar dawrān-i muʿāṣir* (Qum: Intishārāt-i Sarzamīn-i Sabz: 1394 (solar)/2015).

Al-Ālūsī, ʿA., *Rawish-i ʿAllāma Ṭabāṭabā'ī dar Tafsīr al-mīzān*, trans. S.H. Mīr-Jalīlī (Tehran: Markaz-i Chāp wa Nashr-i Sāzmān-i Tablīghāt: 1370 (solar)/1991).

Ayāzī, S.M.ʿA., *al-Mufassirūn ḥayātuhum wa manhajuhum* (Tehran: Nashr-i Wizārat-i Farhang wa Irshād-i Islāmī: 1414 (lunar)/1993).

Bābā'ī, ʿA., *Makātib-i tafsīrī* (Qum: Pajūhishghāh-i Ḥawzih wa Dānishghāh, and Tehran: Samt: 1381 (solar)/2002).

_____ *Qawā'id-i tafsīr-i Qur'ān* (Qum: Pajūhishghāh-i Ḥawzih wa Dānishghāh, and Tehran: Samt: 1394 (solar)/2015).

Al-Dhahabī, M.Ḥ., *al-Tafsīr wa-l-mufassirūn* (Cairo: Dār al-Kutub al-Ḥadītha: 1961).

Gleave, R., *Islam and Literalism* (Edinburgh: Edinburgh University Press: 2013).

Goldziher, I., *Die Richtungen der Islamischen Koranauslegung* (Leiden: Brill: 1920).

_____ *al-Madhāhib al-Islāmiyya fī tafsīr al-Qur'ān*, trans. A. ʿAbd al-Qādir (Cairo: Maṭbaʿat al-ʿUlūm: 1944).

_____ *al-Madhāhib al-Islāmiyya fī tafsīr al-Qurʾān*, trans. A. Al-Najjār (Baghdad: Maktabat al-Khanjī: 1955).

_____ *Girāyish-hā-yi tafsīrī dar miyān-i Musalmānān*, trans. N. Ṭabāṭabāʾī (Tehran: Quqnūs: 1383 (solar)/2004).

_____ *Schools of Koranic Commentators*, trans. W.H. Behn (Wiesbaden: Harrassowitz in Kommission: 2006).

Jawādī-Āmulī, ʿA., *Tasnīm* vol. 1 (Qum: Markaz-i Nashr-i Isrāʾ: 1379 (solar)/2000).

Al-Kulaynī, M., *al-Kāfī* (Qum: Dār al-Ḥadīth: 1429 (lunar)/2008).

Makārim-Shīrāzī, N., *Tafsīr bih raʾy* (Qum: Maṭbūʿātī-yi Hadaf: 1378 (solar)/1988).

Maʿrifat, M.H., *al-Tafsīr wa-l-mufassirūn fī thawbihi al-qashīb* (Mashhad: al-Jāmiʿat al-Raḍawiyya lil-ʿUlūm al-Islāmiyya: 1418 (lunar)/1997).

Miller, D., *Out of Error* (Aldershot: Ashgate: 2006).

Al-Maybudī, M.F., *al-Qawāʾid al-tafsīr ladā l-Shīʿa wa-l-Sunna* (Tehran: al-Majmaʿ al-ʿĀlamī lil-Taqrīb bayn al-Madhāhib al-Islāmiyya: 2007).

Muʾaddab, S.R., *Rawish-hā-yi tafsīr-i Qurʾān* (Tehran: Intishārāt-i Ishrāq: 1380 (solar)/2001).

Paya, A., *Islam, Modernity and a New Millennium: Themes from a Critical Rationalist Reading of Islam* (Taylor and Francis (Kindle Edition): 2018).

_____ *Methods, Methodologies, and Perspectives in the Humanities and Social Sciences: With Particular Reference to Islamic Studies. A Critical Rationalist Interpretation* (London: ICAS Press: 2022).

Pink, J., "Tradition and Ideology in Contemporary Sunnite Qurʾānic Exegesis: Qurʾānic Commentaries from the Arab World, Turkey and Indonesia and their Interpretation of Q. 5:51," in *Die Welt des Islams* 50 (2010a), 3–59.

_____ "Tradition, Authority and Innovation in Contemporary Sunnī Tafsīr: Towards a Typology of Qurʾān Commentaries from the Arab

World, Indonesia and Turkey," in *Journal of Qur'anic Studies* 12 (2010b), 56–82.

Popper, K.R., *The Philosophy of Karl Popper*, ed. Paul Arthur Schilpp, The Library of Living Philosophers (14) (Illinois: Open Court: 1974).

_____ *Objective Knowledge: An Evolutionary Approach* (New York: Oxford University Press Inc: 1979).

_____ *Popper Selections*, ed. David Miller (Princeton: Princeton University Press: 1985).

_____ *The Myth of the Framework: In Defence of Science and Rationality* (London: Routledge: 1994).

Riḍāyī-Isfahānī, M.ʿA., *Manṭiq-i tafsīr-i Qurʾān (1): mabānī wa qawāʾid-i tafsīr-i Qurʾān* (Qum: Markaz-i Bayn al-Milalī-yi Tarjumih wa Nashr-i al-Muṣṭafā (ṣ): 1387 (solar)/2008).

_____ *Manṭiq-i tafsīr-i Qurʾān (2): rawish-hā wa girāyish-hā-yi tafsīrī-yi Qurʾān* (Qum: Markaz-i Bayn al-Milalī-yi Tarjumih wa Nashr-i al-Muṣṭafā (ṣ): 1390 (solar)/2011).

Reza'i Isfahani, M.A., *A Textbook on the Methods of Qur'anic Exegesis* (London: ICAS Press: 2018).

Ṣādiqī, Ḥ., *Dar āmadī-yi naqsh-i dānish-i uṣūl-i fiqh dar tafsīr-i Qurʾān* (Qum: Mu'assisih-yi Āmūzishī wa Pajūhishī-yi Imām Khumaynī: 1391 (solar)/2012).

Ṭabāṭabāʾī, M.H., *al-Mīzān fī tafsīr al-Qurʾān* (Beirut: Mu'assisat al-Aʿlamī lil-Maṭbūʿāt: 1390 (lunar)/1970).

Wansbrough, J.E., *Quranic Studies: Sources and Methods of Scriptural Interpretation* (Oxford: Oxford University Press: 1977).

Zadeh, T., "Quranic Studies and the Literary Turn," in *Journal of the American Oriental Society* 135(2) (2015), pp. 329-342.

Zanjānī, ʿA.ʿA.ʿU., *Mabānī wa rawish-hā-yi tafsīrī-yi Qurʾān* (Tehran: Wizārat-i Farhangī wa Irshād-i Islāmī: 1366 (solar)/1987).

A Textual-Critical Analysis of the Sources of the Duʿāʾ Commencing "Yā man arjūhu li-kulli khayr"

Muḥammad Ghafūrī Nezhād
Associate Professor, Shīʿī Studies Unit
University of Religions and Denominations, Mashhad Branch

Translator's Introduction

It is a pleasure to offer this translation of Professor Ghafūrī Nezhād's study of a Twelver Shīʿī *duʿāʾ* text. The vast corpora of such texts in the Twelver Shīʿī tradition has received extraordinarily little attention in Western academia given its scale and its importance in current and historic practice. Professor Ghafūrī Nezhād's study, by focussing a thorough analysis upon a relatively short *duʿāʾ*, showcases the complexity of how one such text inhabits its context: the vagaries of the *duʿāʾ*'s textual history, the adaptive reception of the text through the centuries, and how that reception engaged with concerns of practice, and how a seemingly innocuous ritual detail connects to a substantial and distinctive discourse within the early Twelver Shīʿī literature concerning devotion and prayer.

I have made a few basic alterations to the original text for purposes of clarity. Most significantly, while Professor Ghafūrī Nezhād includes most of the Arabic texts discussed in full and untranslated, I have largely removed these, retaining the references to where they can be found, in keeping with usual practices of citation. This has necessitated a very few additional points of description within the main text. The textual variations between the different versions of the *duʿāʾ* itself are very minor, and play no part in the article's analysis. As Professor Ghafūrī Nezhād demonstrates, the main points of difference are in the accompanying ritual directions, differences that his article sets out at length. A second, accompanying alteration is my insertion of the whole text of ʿAbbās Qummī's recension of the *duʿāʾ* at the start of the article. The author seems to assume readers' familiarity therewith, while in this translated setting it seems an important point of recourse. Accordingly, occasional references to Qummī's text have been inserted where relevant to the discussion.

George Warner
University of Exeter

ABSTRACT

Amongst the better known *duʿāʾ*s for the month of Rajab is a *duʿāʾ* beginning "You from whom I hope for every good" (*yā man arjūhu li-kulli khayr*), the text and directions for the use of which are included by Shaykh ʿAbbās Qummī in his *Mafātīḥ al-jinān*, cited from Raḍī al-Dīn Ibn Ṭāwūs's *Iqbāl al-aʿmāl*. Ibn Ṭāwūs's text, however, leaves some ambiguity regarding Imam al-Ṣādiq's posture as he recites the *duʿāʾ*, presenting a first avenue for study. As for the text's textual history, an examination of early Imāmī hadith literature reveals that texts resembling this *duʿāʾ* may be found in works including al-Kulaynī's *al-Kāfī*, al-Kashshī's *Rijāl*, and al-Ṭūsī's *Miṣbāḥ al-mutahajjid*, albeit with divergences in their texts, vowelling, and chains of transmission. A survey of this evidence reveals the version in al-Kashshī as bearing the closest resemblance to that given by Ibn Ṭāwūs in *Iqbāl*. In his *Zād al-maʿād*, ʿAllāma al-Majlisī combines the versions of al-Kashshī and *Iqbāl* and, apparently with recourse to the *Kitāb al-duʿāʾ* in *al-Kāfī*, gives his own interpretation of the ambiguous passages in Ibn Ṭāwūs's version. It is this recension in al-Majlisī's *Zād al-maʿād* that underpins current conventions of this *duʿāʾ*'s recital among the Twelver Shīʿī faithful. The following article reveals that, notwithstanding the accuracy of al-Majlisī's exegesis of the obscure parts of

Ibn Ṭāwūs's recension, parts of his interpretation do not fit the text in *Iqbāl*. Analysis of the *duʿā*'s *isnād*, meanwhile, demonstrates that none of the available versions possesses a reliable *isnād*; however, a number of indicators, not least the text's transmission by figures such as al-Kulaynī, al-Kashshī, al-Ṭūsī, and Ibn Ṭāwūs, enable confidence that the thematic core of the text originates with al-Ṣādiq, though the same confidence cannot extent to the textual particularities of any given version (including specifications of when the *duʿā*ʾ should be read, or other ritual directions regarding its recital).

KEYWORDS: *duʿā*ʾ, hadith, *aʿmāl*, al-Majlisī, Ibn Ṭāwūs, ʿAbbās Qummī, Shīʿism

1. Introduction

You from whom I hope for every good	يَا مَنْ أَرْجُوهُ لِكُلِّ خَيْرٍ،
From whose wrath I am safe amidst every wrong	وَآمَنُ سَخَطَهُ عِنْدَ كُلِّ شَرٍّ،
You who give plenty in exchange for pittance	يَا مَنْ يُعْطِي ٱلْكَثِيرَ بِٱلْقَلِيلِ،
You who give to whoever asks	يَا مَنْ يُعْطِي مَنْ سَأَلَهُ
To whoever asks not	يَا مَنْ يُعْطِي مَنْ لَمْ يَسْأَلْهُ
To those who know you not	وَمَنْ لَمْ يَعْرِفْهُ
Even, in your care and mercy,	تَحَنُّناً مِنْهُ وَرَحْمَةً،
Grant me what I ask of you	أَعْطِنِي بِمَسْأَلَتِي إِيَّاكَ
Every good in this world, every good in the next	جَمِيعَ خَيْرِ ٱلدُّنْيَا وَجَمِيعَ خَيْرِ ٱلْآخِرَةِ،

Grant me the protection I ask of you	وَٱصْرِفْ عَنِّي بِمَسْأَلَتِي إِيَّاكَ
From every evil in this world, every evil in the next	جَمِيعَ شَرِّ ٱلدُّنْيَا وَجَمِيعَ شَرِّ ٱلْآخِرَةِ،
For never are you lessened for what you give	فَإِنَّهُ غَيْرُ مَنْقُوصٍ مَا أَعْطَيْتَ،
Grant me ever more of your grace	وَزِدْنِي مِنْ فَضْلِكَ
Generous Lord.	يَا كَرِيمُ.

***

Generous giver, glorious one	يَا ذَا ٱلْجَلَالِ وَٱلْإِكْرَامِ،
Sovereign, gracious one	يَا ذَا ٱلنَّعْمَاءِ وَٱلْجُودِ،
Bestower, powerful one	يَا ذَا ٱلْمَنِّ وَٱلطَّوْلِ،
Keep the fire from my greying hair.[1]	حَرِّمْ شَيْبَتِي عَلَى ٱلنَّارِ.

In his *Mafātīḥ al-jinān*, ʿAbbās Qummī, setting out the daily rites (*aʿmāl*) of the month of Rajab, includes the above *duʿāʾ* cited from Raḍī al-Dīn Ibn Ṭāwūs, which in recent years has become a popular text in Iranian mosques for communal recital after prayer. This *duʿāʾ*, beginning *yā man arjūhu li-kulli khayr* ("You from whom I hope for every good"), has accordingly become a familiar one in many Shīʿī contexts. However, the ritual directions for the *duʿāʾ*'s recital supplied in *Mafātīḥ* (see below) are less widely adhered to, and are at some variance with usual practice. These accompanying ritual directions are somewhat obscure and open to interpretation, and are not understood by the generality of devotees.

Through an examination of the earliest sources of this thematically rich *duʿāʾ* in the hadith literature, this article offers an analysis of the *duʿāʾ*'s text, its chains of transmission, and the ritual directions that accompany it. Is this *duʿāʾ* attested in accepted hadith works, from the

---

1 ʿAbbās Qummī, *Mafātīḥ al-jinān* (Mashhad: Intishārāt-i Āstān-i Quds-i Raḍawī, 1379 Sh./2000), 242-3.

Four Books or the collections of Shaykh al-Ṣadūq?

Is the recital of this *duʿāʾ* indeed specified for the month of Rajab, or can it also be read at other times? What can the sources teach us about the *duʿāʾ*'s text? What ritual details do they afford regarding how it should be recited? When, for example, sources record Imam al-Ṣādiq grasping his beard with his left hand and moving his right index finger left and right, what meaning do these gestures have, and how exactly should they be emulated? Is this posture to be adopted while reciting only the *duʿāʾ*'s final stanzas, or for the entire recital? It is these questions that the following investigation undertakes to answer.

2. Description and Analysis of the *Duʿāʾ*'s Transmission in the Early Source Material

An examination of the hadith literature shows that this *duʿāʾ* is narrated – in different versions – in some of the earliest Shīʿī hadith compendia.

2.1 Al-Kulaynī's Version in *al-Kāfī*

Muḥammad b. Yaʿqūb al-Kulaynī (d. 329/941) narrates a hadith via an unreliable *isnād* from one Abū Jaʿfar (he is identified within the *isnād* only as a man from Kufa who was known by this *kunya* [teknonym]), relating how the latter asked Jaʿfar al-Ṣādiq to teach him a *duʿāʾ*. The Imam replied by teaching him a text that closely resembles the one in *Mafātīḥ*.[2] In this version, however, there is no specification regarding the time of the *duʿāʾ*'s recital, nor are there any accompanying ritual directions, and the *duʿāʾ*'s final lines (from *yā dhā l-jalāli wa-l-ikrām*,

[2] Muḥammad. b. Yaʿqūb al-Kulaynī, *al-Kāfī* (Qom: Dār al-Ḥadīth, 1429/2008), 4:559. Al-Kulaynī transmits the text from Aḥmad b. Muḥammad al-Barqī (d. 274/888 or 280/894) via "several of our companions." According to ʿAllāma al-Ḥillī's (d. 726/1325) assessment, al-Kulaynī's transmitters from al-Barqī include ʿAlī b. Ibrāhīm, ʿAlī b. Muḥammad b. ʿAbdullāh b. Udhayna, Aḥmad b. ʿAbdullāh b. Umayya, and ʿAlī b. al-Ḥasan. Al-Ḥasan b. Yūsuf Ibn al-Muṭahhar al-Ḥillī, *Khulāṣat al-aqwāl*, ed. Muḥammad Ṣādiq Baḥr al-ʿUlūm (Najaf: Dār al-Dhakhāʾir, 1411/1990), 272.

"Generous giver", onwards) are not present.

2.2 Al-Kashshī's Version

In his entry on Bashīr al-Nabbāl, Shajara, and Muḥammad b. Zayd al-Shiḥām, Muḥammad b. ʿUmar al-Kashshī (d. c. 340/951) includes a quite a lengthy story narrated by Muḥammad b. Zayd al-Shiḥām, telling of how Imam al-Ṣādiq once invited him to his house, and of the Imam's great hospitality towards him. The narration goes on to relate how Muḥammad requested that the Imam teach him a *duʿāʾ*, whereupon the Imam dictates to him a *duʿāʾ* very similar to that found in *al-Kāfī*. The narration does not specify any set time for the *duʿāʾ*'s recital, but does include a version of the final lines that al-Kulaynī's text omits. In addition, the text notes that the Imam raised his hands as he recited this last part of the *duʿāʾ*, before placing his hand on his beard, which he did not then move until it was soaked with tears.[3]

The narration is unreliable for a number of reasons, among them that the narrator, Ṭāhir b. ʿĪsā al-Warrāq, is deemed untrustworthy (*ḍaʿīf*). He is one of al-Kashshī's teachers, but an unreliable source of hadith.[4]

2.3 Al-Ṭūsī's Version in *Miṣbāḥ*

In *Miṣbāḥ al-mutahajjid,* in a section outlining supererogatory prayers on Fridays for requesting a particular need (*ḥāja*), Muḥammad b. al-Ḥasan al-Ṭūsī (d. 460/1067) supplies a lengthy programme of devotion in a *mursal* hadith from Imam al-Hādī.[5] Among the *duʿāʾ*s included in this programme, one incorporates a version of the *yā man arjūhu li-kulli*

---

[3] Muḥammad b. ʿUmar al-Kashshī, *Ikhtiyār maʿrifat al-rijāl* (*Rijāl al-Kashshī*), ed. Ḥasan Muṣṭafawī (Mashhad: Muʾassasa-yi Nashr-i Dānishgāh-i Mashhad, 1409/1998), 369-70.

[4] See Muḥammad b. al-Ḥasan al-Ṭūsī, *al-Rijāl* (*Rijāl al-Ṭūsī*), ed. Jawād Qayyūmī Iṣfahānī (Qom: Muʾassasat al-Nashr al-Islāmī, 1373 Sh./1994), 428.

[5] Ibid; *Miṣbāḥ al-mutahajjid wa silāḥ al-mutaʿabbid* (Beirut: Muʾassasat Fiqh al-Shīʿa, 1411/1990), 1:342-57.

khayr duʿāʾ.[6] In addition, elsewhere in *Miṣbāḥ* under the heading "*Duʿāʾ* for Recital Following the Six *Rakaʿāt* After Midday Prayers" is a set of *duʿāʾ*s without *isnād*s, including another text very similar to the *duʿāʾ* under discussion.[7]

2.4 Ibn Ṭāwūs's Version in *Iqbāl*

The version of the *duʿāʾ* in Raḍī al-Dīn Ibn Ṭāwūs's (d. 664/1266) *Iqbāl al-aʿmāl* differs from those of al-Kulaynī, al-Kashshī, and al-Ṭūsī in terms of its *isnād*, its text (albeit not substantially), and the ritual instructions attached to its recitation. In this version, al-Ṣādiq's interlocutor is Muḥammad b. Dhakwān, nicknamed al-Sajjād – "the worshipful; the one who prostrates frequently". Ibn Ṭāwūs's source for the tradition, identified as al-Ṭirāzī, cites a number of sources to the effect that Muḥammad b. Dhakwān acquired this epithet due to his long prostrations in prayer and his copious weeping in prostration, which ultimately rendered him blind.

Another distinguishing feature of Ibn Ṭāwūs's text in *Iqbāl* is that the Imam's interlocutor mentions while requesting the *duʿāʾ* that it is the month of Rajab, and specifically asks that the Imam teach him a *duʿāʾ* that will ensure God's blessings when recited during that month. Accordingly, before dictating the *duʿāʾ* itself, the Imam commands, "Every day of the month of Rajab, morning and evening, and after each of your prayers day and night, recite [this *duʿāʾ*]."[8]

Ibn Ṭāwūs's *Iqbāl* is thus the earliest surviving testimony to a link

---

[6] Ibid., 1:353. This version of the *duʿāʾ* is identical to one included in Ibn Ṭāwūs's *Jamāl al-usbūʿ*, save for a short additional phrase in the latter, a discrepancy that can be ascribed to scribal error. See Raḍī al-Dīn ʿAlī b. Mūsā Ibn Ṭāwūs, *Jamāl al-usbūʿ bi-kamāl al-ʿamal al-mashrūʿ* (Qom: Dār al-Raḍī, 1330/1911), 378-9.

[7] See al-Ṭūsī, *Miṣbāḥ al-mutahajjid*, 1:378; Also see Ibn Ṭāwūs, *Jamāl al-usbūʿ*, 438.

[8] Ibn Ṭāwūs, *al-Iqbāl bi-l-aʿmāl*, ed. Jawād Qayyūmī Iṣfahānī (Qom: Daftar-i Tablīghāt-i Islāmī, 1376Sh./1997), 3:211.

between this *du'ā'* and the month of Rajab. According to this version, al-Ṣādiq, after reciting the line *wa-zidnī min faḍlika yā karīm* ("Grant me ever more of your grace, Generous Lord"), raises his left hand to grasp his beard. He then recites the *du'ā'* a second time, while appealing to God with a gesture of his right index finger (*wa-huwa yalūdhu bi-sabbābatihi al-yumnā*). It would appear that in this second recital, having dictated the text to his interlocutor, the Imam now ponders more deeply upon the contents of the *du'ā'*. He then dictates the final few phrases of the *du'ā'*, from "Generous giver" to the end. These details are all reproduced almost verbatim in Qummī's *Mafātīḥ*. Ibn Ṭāwūs then ends the text with the following detail:

In another narration, it is stated that the Imam took his beard in his hand after reading the *du'ā'*, keeping it there until the back of the hand was soaked with tears.

This could be a reference to al-Kashshī's text, as described above.[9] Al-Majlisī, meanwhile, transmits this text in *Biḥār* exactly as it appears in *Iqbāl*.[10]

Ibn Ṭāwūs's version prompts two avenues of inquiry: first, what is the relationship between his version and that of al-Kashshī? Second, what is the state of the *isnād* used by Ibn Ṭāwūs?

2.4.1 Comparing the Versions of Ibn Ṭāwūs and al-Kashshī

Could the texts presented by Ibn Ṭāwūs and al-Kashshī originate from a single source text, both portraying the same encounter? A first difference to note concerns the settings in which the two authors' accounts introduce the *du'ā'*. Al-Kashshī supplies a frame narrative which is several lines in length, recounting in some detail the narrator's several meetings with the Imam, ostensibly in Medina, and how these

---

[9] See al-Kashshī, *Rijāl*, 369-70.

[10] Muḥammad Bāqir al-Majlisī, *Biḥār al-anwār* (Beirut: Dār Iḥyā' al-Turāth al-'Arabī, 1403/1983), 95:390-1.

came about. Ibn Ṭāwūs's version, by contrast, gives no such account of multiple meetings; instead, more detailed attention is paid to matters such as when exactly the *du'ā'* should be read, and the Imam's behaviour at different points during his recital of the *du'ā'*. These differences, however, may easily be explained by the fact that these two versions are found in two different kinds of book: al-Kashshī's is a *rijāl* work, while both Ibn Ṭāwūs's *Iqbāl* and the book of al-Ṭirāzī that he cites are collections of *du'ā'* texts. Thus far, then, a shared source remains plausible.

This possibility recedes, however, when we consider another significant detail of these texts, namely the differences in their *isnād*s and in the first links thereof in particular.

In al-Kashshī's text, the Imam teaches the *du'ā'* to Muḥammad b. Zayd al-Shiḥām, while in *Iqbāl* the Imam's interlocutor is Muḥammad b. Dhakwān al-Sajjād. In both versions, the second link in the *isnād* is Muḥammad b. Sinān. While one could reasonably hypothesise a confusion between "Shiḥām" and "Sajjād" originating from a scribal error, such a confusion between "Dhakwān" and "Zayd" is scarcely plausible, notwithstanding some scholars of *rijāl* having suggested as much.[11] Muḥaqqiq Muḥammad Taqī Shūshtarī (d. 1995) suggests that both names are a corruption of "Ziyād" on the basis that al-Ṭūsī names one Muḥammad b. Ziyād al-Sajjād al-Ghazzāl as a companion of Ja'far al-Ṣādiq, and states that Muḥammad b. Sinān transmitted from him.[12]

Thus, he proposes, two separate errors could have rendered "Ziyād" respectively into "Zayd" and into "Dhakwān". Elsewhere, Shūshtarī points to the lack of an entry for Muḥammad b. Dhakwān al-Sajjād in al-Ṭūsī's *Rijāl* as evidence that the name originates from the corruption of another; certainly, al-Ṭūsī's criteria for inclusion in his *Rijāl* would

---

[11] This opinion is shared by 'Abdullāh Māmaqānī (d. 1933), who writes, "I do not consider probable a confusion here between Dhakwān and Zayd. God knows best." See 'Abdullāh Māmaqānī, *Tanqīḥ al-maqāl fī 'ilm al-rijāl* (np., nd.), 3:115.

[12] Al-Ṭūsī, *Rijāl*, 283; Muḥammad Taqī Shūshtarī, *Qāmūs al-rijāl* (Qom: Mu'assasat al-Nashr al-Islāmī, 1410/1989), 9:260.

usually have covered Ibn Dhakwān had he existed.[13] In another passage, Shūshtarī contends the probable validity of "Muḥammad b. Ziyād al-Sajjād" on the basis that it is less likely than the other two names to have been the outcome of scribal confusion.[14] Shūshtarī's fundamental point is that of these three names, only "Ziyād" could plausibly have engendered both of the other two through scribal error; thus, a confusion between "Zayd" and "Dhakwān" is improbable, while both "Zayd" and "Dhakwān" could conceivably both be corruptions of "Ziyād". It is Ziyād, accordingly, that he identifies as the original name.

It is important to note that neither Muḥammad b. Zayd al-Shiḥām nor Muḥammad al-Shiḥām are found in the *isnād*s of the Four Books or those of al-Ḥurr al-ʿĀmilī's (d. 1104/1693) *Wasāʾil al-Shīʿa*, nor is either name found in other early books of *rijāl* except for this one instance of his being narrated from by al-Kashshī, which only attests to the latter's positive assessment of his character. Muḥammad b. Zayd, meanwhile, occurs a total of five times in the *isnād*s of these works, though this has not led to his being considered in the *rijāl* literature.

As for Muḥammad b. Dhakwān, this name is not found in the early *rijāl* literature, nor in the *isnād*s of the Four Books or of *Wasāʾil*. He does appear four times in the *isnād*s of Shaykh al-Ṣadūq's (d. 381/991) writings, though he is not referred to as "al-Sajjād" in any of these instances.[15] He is also absent from early *rijāl* literature. As for a Muḥammad b. Ziyād bearing the epithet "al-Sajjād", he only appears in al-Ṭūsī's *Rijāl* as remarked above, without any testament to his soundness as a narrator.[16]

---

[13] Shūshtarī, *Qāmūs al-rijāl*, 9:275.

[14] Ibid., 9:272.

[15] See Muḥammad b. ʿAlī Ibn Bābawayh al-Shaykh al-Ṣadūq, *al-Amālī* (Tehran: Kitābchī, 1376 Sh./1997), 330; ibid., *ʿUyūn akhbār al-Riḍā* (Tehran: Intishārāt-i Jahān, 1378/1958), 1:250; ibid., *Kamāl al-dīn wa tamām al-niʿma*, ed. ʿAlī Akbar Ghaffārī (Tehran: Dār al-Kutub al-Islāmiyya, 1395/1975), 1:68, 272; see also ʿAlī Namāzī Shāhrūdī, *Mustadrakāt ʿilm rijāl al-ḥadīth* (Tehran: Farzand-i Muʾallif, 1414/1993), 7:91.

[16] See al-Ṭūsī, *Rijāl*, 283.

Overall, it is clear that none of the three potential narrators of this hadith can be relied upon, according to the standards established in the *rijāl* literature.

2.4.2 Analysing Ibn Ṭāwūs's *Isnād*

As has already been mentioned, Ibn Ṭāwūs cites his version of the *duʿā'* from a book (*kitāb*) compiled by one Muḥammad b. ʿAlī al-Ṭirāzī.[17] Al-Ṭirāzī, in turn, transmits the text through an *isnād* comprising the following individuals: his immediate source, Abū l-Ḥasan ʿAlī b. Muḥammad al-Bursī (upon whom al-Ṭirāzī invokes God's blessing), al-Ḥusayn b. Aḥmad b. Shaybān, Ḥamza b. al-Qāsim al-ʿAlawī al-ʿAbbāsī, Muḥammad b. ʿAbdullāh b. ʿImrān al-Barqī, Muḥammad b. ʿAlī al-Hamadānī, and Muḥammad b. Sinān, a companion of Jaʿfar al-Ṣādiq who transmits the hadith from the Imam's interlocutor therein, one Muḥammad al-Sajjād. Muḥammad b. Sinān also notes that this text is only part of a longer hadith.[18] The next step of our analysis, then, must be to discuss al-Ṭirāzī and the book in which he included this hadith, and then to examine the *isnād* whereby he traces it back to al-Ṣādiq.

2.4.2.1 Muḥammad b. ʿAlī al-Ṭirāzī and his *Kitāb*

The early *rijāl* works and bibliographical literature yield no information on al-Ṭirāzī or his book; our only knowledge comes from what Ibn Ṭāwūs tells us in *Iqbāl* and some details in Muḥammad Bāqir al-Majlisī's (d. 1110/1699) *Jamāl al-usbūʿ*. Turning to later *rijāl* literature, however, affords us a further account of al-Ṭirāzī and his family assembled by Āqā Buzurg Tihrānī (d. 1970).

Drawing on al-Khaṭīb al-Baghdādī's (d. 463/1071) entry on al-Ṭirāzī's grandfather Abū Bakr al-Ṭirāzī, Tihrānī reconstructs his genealogy as

[17] Māmaqānī sets the pronunciation of his name as al-Ṭirāzī, identifying three locations to which such a toponym could relate: an area of Marv, an area of Isfahan, and a chilly city within the Turkic speaking regions. Māmaqānī, *Tanqīḥ*, 3:157.

[18] Ibn Ṭāwūs, *Iqbāl*, 3:211-12.

follows: "Muḥammad b. Abī l-Ḥasan ʿAlī b. Abī Bakr Muḥammad b. Muḥammad b. Aḥmad b. ʿUthmān b. Aḥmad al-Baghdādī, known as al-Ṭirāzī." Al-Baghdādī narrates from al-Ṭirāzī's grandfather (Abū Bakr Muḥammad) via his father (Abū l-Ḥasan ʿAlī), thus identifying the latter as one of al-Baghdādī's teachers.

Furthermore, on the basis of Ibn Ṭāwūs's citations from al-Ṭirāzī's book, Tihrānī identifies a number of al-Ṭirāzī's teachers, including Abū l-Faraj Qazwīnī, Abū l-ʿAbbās Aḥmad b. ʿAlī b. Nūḥ, Muḥammad b. Hārūn b. Mūsā al-Tallʿukbarī, and Abū Muḥammad ʿAbdullāh b. al-Ḥusayn b. Yaʿqūb al-Fārsī. From this we learn that al-Ṭirāzī moved in the same circles as al-Ṭūsī and Aḥmad b. ʿAlī al-Najāshī (d. 450/1058 or after 463/1070). In addition, Tihrānī gives the title of al-Ṭirāzī's book as *Kitāb al-duʿāʾ wa-l-ziyāra*.[19]

A comprehensive analysis of Ibn Ṭāwūs's citations of al-Ṭirāzī, of which there are twenty-three in total, gives a clearer picture of his scholarly character, the principal elements of which are as follows:[20] notwithstanding the fact that al-Ṭirāzī's father and grandfather were known to Sunnī scholars during their lifetimes, the surviving contents of al-Ṭirāzī's book are of a pronouncedly Shīʿī character, such that non-Shīʿīs would be highly unlikely to have transmitted them. Indeed, his extant writings suggest an inclination towards maximalist (so-called "extremist") currents within the Imāmiyya.

The texts transmitted from him by Ibn Ṭāwūs are mostly traced back to the Imams themselves or to prominent Imāmīs – figures from whom non-Imāmīs do not narrate. These include twelve narrations from

---

19 Āqā Buzurg Muḥammad Muḥsin Tihrānī, *al-Dharīʿa ilā taṣānīf al-Shīʿa* (Beirut: Dār al-Aḍwāʾ, 1403/1982), 8:195-6. For al-Ṭirāzī see also Māmaqānī, *Tanqīḥ*, 3:157-8; Shāhrūdī, *Mustadrakāt*, 7:234, 244; Shūshtarī, *Qāmūs*, 9:451; Abū l-Qāsim al-Khoei, *Muʿjam rijāl al-ḥadīth wa tafṣīl tabaqāt al-ruwāt* (London: Muʾassasat al-Imām al-Khūʾī al-Islāmiyya, nd.), 18:55.

20 In a forthcoming publication, I examine the figure of al-Ṭirāzī and his *kitāb* in more detail.

Imam al-Ṣādiq,[21] one text each from Imams al-Sajjād[22] and al-Kāẓim,[23] and three from Imam al-Jawād,[24] as well as a text from al-Ḥusayn b. Rawḥ al-Nawbakhtī, the third emissary of the Twelfth Imam.[25] Al-Ṭirāzī, Ibn Ṭāwūs tells us, also possessed a document written by Muḥammad b. Hārūn b. Mūsā l-Tallʿukbarī (d. 385/995) attesting to his father's excellent standing amongst the Imāmiyya.[26]

Furthermore, Ibn Ṭāwūs includes al-Ṭirāzī alongside figures like al-Kulaynī, al-Ṣadūq, Shaykh al-Mufīd (d. 413/1022), and al-Ṭūsī among "those possessed of plenteous virtue" (*dhawū l-faḍl al-kathīr*).[27] More broadly, he refers to al-Ṭirāzī in respectful terms, referring to him several times as *shaykh*[28] and calling God's mercy upon him, as befitting an esteemed forbear.[29] Such indications of Ibn Ṭāwūs's high regard for al-Ṭirāzī, and the fact that he kept the latter's *kitāb* to hand and makes frequent citations thereof in *Iqbāl*, leave little doubt that this book contained nothing that Ibn Ṭāwūs found objectionable, and that he considered al-Ṭirāzī a trustworthy scholar. Moreover, in eight of his twenty-three citations of al-Ṭirāzī, Ibn Ṭāwūs is able to access the same hadith that he quotes from al-Ṭirāzī through an alternative *isnād*, further bolstering our impression of al-Ṭirāzī as a reliable source.

Though the above evidence establishes al-Ṭirāzī as a trusted source, the difficulty remains that none of these twenty-three citations is accompanied by any discussion of the chain of authority linking the

[21] See Ibn Ṭāwūs, *Iqbāl*, 1:266, 2:70, 264, 276, 279, 282, 3:209, 210, 229, 232, 265, 268, 317.

[22] Ibid., 3:299.

[23] Ibid., 3:276.

[24] Ibid., 3:265.

[25] Ibid., 3:272.

[26] Ibid., 3:347.

[27] Ibid., 2:263-4.

[28] Ibn Ṭāwūs, *Jamāl al-usbūʿ*, 32.

[29] Ibid., *Iqbāl*, 3:272.

two scholars, even while Ibn Ṭāwūs is separated from al-Ṭirāzī by some two centuries. The evidence makes plain that Ibn Ṭāwūs is accessing al-Ṭirāzī's book through written transmission.[30] Ibn Ṭāwūs does state twice that he had at his disposal an autograph manuscript of the book,[31] but this claim is evidently guesswork. A further locus of uncertainty is the title of al-Ṭirāzī's book, which is once given in *Iqbāl* as *al-Riwāyāt al-shāhidāt lil-saʿādāt bi-l-ʿibādāt*.[32] Tihrānī, as noted, gives a different title, *Kitāb al-duʿāʾ wa-l-ziyāra*, but this seems improbable.[33] Etan Kohlberg, meanwhile, stops short of a firm conclusion on the point.[34]

2.4.2.2 Al-Ṭirāzī's Chain of Transmission from Jaʿfar al-Ṣādiq

Al-Ṭirāzī's immediate source for the hadith containing the *duʿāʾ* under discussion is Abū l-Ḥasan ʿAlī b. Muḥammad al-Bursī – his given *isnād* thus begins: "Abū l-Ḥasan ʿAlī b. Muḥammad al-Bursī (may God be pleased with him) narrates (*rawā*) ..."; the benediction following al-Bursī's name indicates that al-Ṭirāzī knew him personally. However, his use of *rawā* when transmitting from al-Bursī, rather than *akhbaranā* or *ḥaddathanā*, indicates that al-Ṭirāzī was not authorised by al-Bursī to narrate hadith from him. Early *rijāl* works do not mention al-Bursī, while later and contemporary *rijāl* scholars supply no more information than the contents of the citations in *Iqbāl*.

Several scholars have read the benedictions after al-Bursī's name as originating with Ibn Ṭāwūs and not al-Ṭirāzī, perhaps thereby seeking to

---

[30] See, for example, Ibn Ṭāwūs, *Iqbāl*, 3:299.

[31] Ibid., 3:299, 347.

[32] Ibid., 3:232.

[33] Tihrānī, *al-Dharīʿa*, 8:195.

[34] Etan Kohlberg, *Kitābkhāna-yi Ibn-i Ṭāwūs wa aḥwāl wa āthār-i ū*, trans. Rasul Jafarian and ʿAlī Quli Qarai (Qom: Kitābkhāna-yi ʿUmūmī-yi Ḥaḍrat-i Āyatullāh al-ʿUẓmā Marʿashī Najafī, 1371 Sh./1992), 246.

affirm al-Bursī's reliability as a narrator.[35] Tihrānī, meanwhile, cautions that al-Bursī is not to be confused with Abū l-Ḥasan ʿAlī b. Muḥammad al-Qurashī (d. 348/959). Al-Qurashī was a teacher of Aḥmad b. ʿAbd al-Wāḥid, who, in turn, was a teacher of both al-Ṭūsī and al-Najāshī, scholars who were al-Ṭirāzī's contemporaries, in Tihrānī's assessment, and who moved in similar circles.[36] In sum, the *rijāl* literature does not validate al-Bursī as a reliable source, nor are any indicators of his reliability forthcoming from the wider source material.

Since it has already become apparent that the narrator of this hadith from the Imam himself is identified by a number of different names, none of which are confirmed as reliable persons, there is no benefit in further analysing other links in the *isnād*.

2.5 Al-Majlisī's Version in *Zād al-maʿād*

As already noted, al-Majlisī includes Ibn Ṭāwūs's version of the *duʿāʾ* in *Biḥār* without any alterations. In *Zād al-maʿād*, however, he leaves out Ibn Ṭāwūs's and al-Ṭirāzī's introductory remarks, as well as al-Ṭirāzī's *isnād* up to Muḥammad b. Dhakwān, stating only that "It is narrated from Muḥammad b. Dhakwān via a credible (*muʿtabar*) *isnād* ..." That al-Majlisī deems the *isnād* credible is probably an expression of his Akhbārī outlook; the Akhbārīs generally took such a view of any narrations found in well-established books. Al-Majlisī then gives the text of the *duʿāʾ* itself and the dialogue between al-Ṣādiq and the narrator and as they appear in *Iqbāl*, except that he follows the line "Grant me ever more of your grace, Generous Lord" with the following: "[The Imam] then grasped his noble beard with his left hand, meanwhile moving his right index finger left and right, reciting this *duʿāʾ*,"[37] then giving the final phrases of

[35] See Māmaqānī, *Tanqīḥ*, 2:303; Shāhrūdī, *Mustadrakāt*, 5:439; see also Shūshtarī, *Qāmūs*, 7:543.

[36] Tihrānī, *abaqāt aʿlām al-Shīʿa* (Beirut: Dār Iḥyāʾ al-Turāth al-ʿArabī, 1430/2008), 2:175-6.

[37] Al-Majlisī, *Zād al-maʿād wa miftāḥ al-jinān*, ed. ʿAlāʾ al-Dīn al-Aʿlamī (Beirut: Muʾassasat al-Aʿlamī lil-Maṭbūʿāt, 1423/2002), 16-17.

the *duʿāʾ* as they appear in *Iqbāl* and in Qummī's *Mafātīḥ*.

There emerge here a number of divergences between al-Majlisī's text and that of Ibn Ṭāwūs.

First, al-Ṣādiq in al-Majlisī's version adopts his noted posture (grasping his beard and appealing to God with a gesture of his right index finger) as he recites the *duʿāʾ*'s final lines, whereas Ibn Ṭāwūs's text seems to state that the Imam recites the whole *duʿāʾ* a second time once Muḥammad b. Dhakwān has written it down, and adopts his new posture for the whole of this second recital. This discrepancy may result from al-Majlisī's amending the text based upon al-Kashshī's version; the latter describes the Imam raising his hands as he recites the final phrases of the *duʿāʾ*.

The second discrepancy concerns the phrase in Ibn Ṭāwūs's text "appealing to God with a gesture (*yalūdhu* – see below) of his right index finger," which in al-Majlisī's version is replaced with "moving (*yuḥarriku*) his right index finger left and right." This may well be a case of al-Majlisī seeking to clarify what is a somewhat obscure phrase in the earlier version.

A third difference is al-Majlisī's apparent merging of the versions of Ibn Ṭāwūs and al-Kashshī at the end of the text, giving "He continued until [his hand] was wet with tears," which has a similar sense to al-Kashshī's text, though the two are not identical. Al-Kashshī's version, after the Imam has recited the entire *duʿāʾ*, states as follows: "He then placed his hand on his beard, keeping it there until the back of the hand was soaked with his tears."[38]

A first conclusion of these observations is that it is al-Majlisī's *Zād al-maʿād* that is the historical source of the ritual accompaniments with which some Shīʿīs today recite this *duʿāʾ* – these are much closer to what al-Majlisī describes than to those in *Mafātīḥ*, which reproduces the text of *Iqbāl* as described above. It remains to ask to what extent al-Majlisī's gloss of the phrase "*wa-huwa yalūdhu bi-sabbābatihi al-yumnā*," which

---

[38] Al-Kashshī, *Rijāl*, 370.

he interprets as denoting a left-right movement of the index finger, is correct. What is the meaning of this text, which first appears Ibn Ṭāwūs's transmission from al-Ṭirāzī, and what does it portend?

3. The Phrase *"yalūdhu bi-sabbābatihi"* and its Meaning

One possible explanation for this passage is that it denotes a customary expression of vehement supplication current in the Arabian Peninsula at the time of the hadith's origin. An alternative possibility is that it is not solely a manifestation of local custom, instead constituting a legal direction on the part of the Imam. Determining which is correct requires a consultation of the linguistic data in conjunction with an analysis of the Shīʿī hadith corpus.

3.1 Linguistic Analysis of *l-w-dh*

A diachronic survey of various linguistic and lexicographical works yields a number of meanings for the root *l-w-dh* as follows: "to be concealed", "to seek shelter", "to take refuge",[39] "to adhere", "to seek help".[40] Ibn Fāris (d. 395/1004) denotes the core meaning of this root as being "to circle around something and to seek refuge therewith through fear or greed."[41]

[39] Khalīl b. Aḥmad Farāhīdī, *Kitāb al-ʿayn* (Qom: Intishārāt-i Hijrat, 1409/1998), 8:199; Muḥammad b. Aḥmad al-Azharī, *Tahdhīb al-lugha* (Beirut: Dār Iḥyāʾ al-Turāth al-ʿArabī, 1421/2000), 15:13; al-Ṣāḥib Ibn ʿAbbād, *al-Muḥīṭ fī l-lugha*, ed. Muḥammad Ḥasan Āl Yāsīn (Beirut: ʿĀlam al-Kutub, 1414/1994), 10:101; Ismāʿīl b. Ḥammād al-Jawharī, *al-Ṣiḥāḥ*, ed. Aḥmad ʿAbd al-Ghafūr ʿAṭṭār (Beirut: Dār al-ʿIlm lil-Malāyīn, 1376/1956), 2:570; Maḥmūd b. ʿUmar Zamakhsharī, *Muqaddimat al-adab* (Tehran: Muʾassasa-yi Muṭālaʿāt-i Islāmī-yi Dānishgāh-i Tihrān, 1386 Sh./2007), 143; Muḥammad b. Mukarram Ibn Manẓūr, *Lisān al-ʿArab* (Beirut: Dār Ṣādir, 1414/1993), 3:507; Aḥmad b. Muḥammad al-Fayyūmī, *al-Miṣbāḥ al-munīr fī gharīb al-Sharḥ al-kabīr lil-Rāfiʿī* (Qom: Dār al-Hijra, 1414/1993), 560; Muḥammad b. Muḥammad al-Zabīdī, *Tāj al-ʿarūs min jawāhir al-qāmūs* (Beirut: Dār al-Fikr, 1414/1993), 5:394.

[40] Al-Mubārak b. Muḥammad Ibn al-Athīr, *al-Nihāya fī gharīb al-ḥadīth wa-l-athar* (Qom: Muʾassasat Ismāʿīlīyān, 1367 Sh./1988), 4:276.

[41] Aḥmad Ibn Fāris, *Muʿjam maqāyīs al-lugha* (Qom: Maktab al-Iʿlām al-Islāmī, 1404/1983), 5:220; see also Muḥammad b. al-Ḥasan Ibn Durayd, *Jamharat al-*

The contemporary scholar al-Muṣṭafawī, meanwhile, defines *l-w-dh* as denoting "approaching something and joining therewith in pursuit of a specific aim."[42]

The lexicographical literature thus does not support a meaning of *l-w-dh* that directly involves the index finger. Such an interpretation is only suggested by Fakhr al-Dīn al-Ṭurayḥī (d. 1085/1674) in his *Majma' al-baḥrayn*, a lexicon of obscure terms in the Qur'an and hadith literature in which we find the following: "To '*lādha*' with the index finger, is to express self-abasement (*taḍarra'a*) by moving one's index finger."[43]

Al-Ṭurayḥī is known as a scholar of lexicographically difficult hadith, and indeed may be considered the first Twelver Shī'ī scholar to write specifically on this topic. This being the case, it is highly likely that al-Ṭurayḥī's basis for this meaning of *l-w-dh* is a group of hadiths concerning the terms *taḍarru'* and *tabattul*, several of which can be found in al-Kulaynī's *al-Kāfī*, and which shall be discussed in the next section.

In the course of the above investigation, it has become apparent that usages of the root *l-w-dh* involving the index finger (*lādha bi-sabbābatihi*) were not widespread in the early Islamic centuries. In what follows, however, we shall see how a conjunction between specific movements of the index finger and expressions of seeking shelter, appealing for refuge, and self-abasement is observable in early Shī'ī discourses through the teachings of Ja'far al-Ṣādiq, particularly with reference to the exegesis of certain Qur'anic terms.

lugha (Beirut: np., 1988), 2:702.

[42] Ḥasan al-Muṣṭafawī, *al-Taḥqīq fī kalimāt al-Qur'ān al-karīm* (Beirut, Cairo, London: Markaz Nashr Āthār al-'Allāma al-Muṣṭafawī, 1430/2008), 10:283.

[43] Fakhr al-Dīn b. Muḥammad al-Ṭurayḥī, *Majma' al-baḥrayn* (Tehran: al-Maktaba al-Murtaḍawiyya, 1375 Sh./1996), 3:188.

3.2 Supplication and Gesture in the Early Shīʿī Hadith Corpus

The fourteenth chapter of al-Kulaynī's *Kitāb al-duʿāʾ* in *al-Kāfī*, entitled *al-Raghba wa-l-rahba wa-l-taḍarruʿ wa-l-tabattul wa-l-ibtihāl wa-l-istiʿādha wa-l-masʾala* (for translation see below), contains seven hadiths addressing various aspects of *duʿāʾ* and proper supplication before God.[44]

1. In the chapter's first hadith – which is classed as weak due to the presence of an unknown narrator, one Abū Isḥāq, in the *isnād* – Imam al-Ṣādiq identifies holding the palms of the hands towards the sky as denoting *raghba* (yearning) for God, and identifies holding the backs of the hands towards the sky as denoting *rahba* (fear) of God. The Imam then gives an exegesis of Q 73:8: "So remember the name of your Lord and devote yourself wholly to Him" (*wa-dhkur isma rabbika wa-tabattal ilayhi tabtīlan*), declaring that *tabtīl* (exclusive devotion) refers to supplicating God whilst gesturing with one finger. He further states that *taḍarruʿ* (self-abasement) involves making supplication while gesturing with two fingers, while *ibtihāl* (pleading) comprises the holding of both hands aloft while weeping. One may interpret the hadith as identifying *tabattul* (devotion) as *duʿāʾ*, an act that it divides into three stages: first, a supplicating gesture involving one finger; second, a gesture with two fingers, sometimes labelled *taḍarruʿ*; third, stretching out the hands and weeping, which the Imam terms *ibtihāl*.

2. In the chapter's second and sixth narrations (transmitted reliably from Muḥammad b. Muslim), Imam al-Bāqir interprets two terms: *istikāna* (humility) is defined as *khuḍūʿ* (a near-synonym), and *taḍarruʿ* as the raising of both hands whilst sobbing.

3. In the third narration – this time with an interrupted (*mursal*) *isnād* – al-Ṣādiq identifies *taḍarruʿ* as moving the fingers left and right, *tabattul* as moving the fingers up and down, and *ibtihāl* as raising the hands in front of one's face and turning to face the *qibla*, adding that

[44] Al-Kulaynī, *al-Kāfī*, 4:323-7.

ibtihāl is not realised until the eyes flow with tears.

4. In the fourth hadith, narrated reliably (*ṣaḥīḥ*) from Muḥammad b. Muslim, al-Ṣādiq identifies *taḍarruʿ* as moving the right index finger left and right, *tabattul* as moving the left index finger up and down, and *ibtihāl* as raising the hands towards the sky.

5. The fifth hadith is considered weak due to its acknowledged uncertainty regarding whether Aḥmad al-Barqī transmits the text from his father or someone else. In this hadith, al-Ṣādiq states that *tabattul* is gesturing with the index finger, *ibtihāl* is raising the hands above one's head, and *taḍarruʿ* is moving the index finger in front of one's face. This is further identified as *duʿāʾ al-khīfa* – "the *duʿāʾ* of fear".

6. The chapter's seventh hadith is reliably narrated by al-Ṣādiq's disciples Muḥammad b. Muslim and Zurāra. In response to their question, the Imam states that *masʾala* (making a request)[45] is performed with the palms of the hands open, *istiʿādha* (taking refuge) is the raising of both hands with the palms upwards, *tabattul* is pointing with the finger, and *taḍarruʿ* is moving the finger.

An important element of this chapter's hadith is the fact that the terms singled out for interpretation therein are Qur'anic terms. In several instances, moreover, the terms appear in the Qur'anic text as the object of divine command – states or attitudes that the Qur'an's audience are exhorted to adopt.

3.3 Schematic Analysis of al-Kulaynī's Hadith

Synthesising the content of these hadiths from *al-Kāfī* (disregarding their *isnād*s), one arrives at a schema whereby moving or gesturing with the finger(s) while making supplication to God may be categorised as follows:

1. Pointing with one finger: *tabattul* (hadith 1).
2. Moving and pointing with two fingers: *taḍarruʿ* (hadith 1).

[45] Translator's note: the author gives "*suʾāl*" here in the Persian, but the text of the hadith is "*masʾala*".

3. Moving the fingers left and right: *taḍarruʿ* (hadith 3).
4. Moving the fingers up and down: *tabattul* (hadith 3).
5. Moving the right index finger left and right: *taḍarruʿ* (hadith 4).
6. Moving the left index finger up and down: *tabattul* (hadith 4).
7. Pointing with the index finger: *tabattul* (hadith 5).
8. Moving the index finger in front of one's face: *khīfa* (hadith 5).

Among these eight categories, notwithstanding the probable overlap between them, those most pertinent to the phrase "*wa huwa yalūdhu bisabbābatihi*" are numbers one, five, seven, and eight. In addition, the movements described in number five can both encompass the contents of numbers one and seven, and also be included in those described in number eight. In terms of their *isnād*s, meanwhile, the texts supporting numbers one, seven, and eight are quite unreliable; only number five is sound in this regard. There is little doubt that al-Majlisī consulted these hadiths in his interpretation of the phrase in question, and these *isnād*-based considerations likely had an impact upon his choice of the fifth category as the basis for his reading thereof. One should recall, though, that Ibn Ṭāwūs's version of the *duʿāʾ* – upon which al-Majlisī apparently relies – also has an unreliable *isnād*, suggesting that *isnād*-criticism was not generally a decisive factor in al-Majlisī's use of these texts.

It remains the case, meanwhile, that some practical elements of what the fifth category describes are not quite clear. As the index finger is moved, for example, do the hand and forearm remain still, or should the movement be from the wrist or the elbow? The hadiths give no answers. Similarly, there is no indication in which direction the palm of the hand should be facing while the fingers are pointed and/or moved. This being the case, attention should be paid to the shared elements of all these modes of supplication, namely the inner, spiritual state of meek humility before God that the hadiths describing all of the above categories emphasise to varying degrees. Such an inner state would seem to be reflected better in the movement of the arm from the elbow, and with the palms held perpendicular to the ground.

4. Conclusion

The conclusions of the above study are as follows:

1. Despite the *duʿā*'s attestation in several early Shīʿī hadith compendia, none of these attestations furnish it with an *isnād* that meets the criteria for *ṣaḥīḥ* authenticity as defined by the scholars of the school of Ḥilla. Nevertheless, in light of certain indicators within the text of the *duʿāʾ* itself, and of the fact that the text is transmitted by two of the authors of the Four Books, as well as figures like Ibn Ṭāwūs and al-Kashshī, one may be confident that the thematic core of the text originates from the Imams. Such certainty, however, cannot extend to the specifities of the text, including the text's association with any particular time and the ritual details concerning its recitation.
2. Al-Majlisī's interpretation of the phrase *wa-huwa yalūdhu bi-sabbābatihi al-yumnā* fits with what is narrated from Jaʿfar al-Ṣādiq, but is not exhaustive; the Imams' hadith attest to other, different modes of supplication and self-abasement before God involving gesturing with the fingers. It appears that al-Majlisī's specification of these ritual details for the recitation of the *duʿā*'s final lines is synthesised from two separate versions of the text – those transmitted by Ibn Ṭāwūs and al-Kashshī. In Ibn Ṭāwūs's version, the Imam mandates these particularities for performance throughout the *duʿā*'s recital, while al-Kashshī's text has the Imam raising his hands heavenwards only during the last part of the *duʿāʾ*.
3. The texts seem to suggest that the importance of one's inner condition, striving for a state of humility and self-abasement before God, and making supplication to Him with complete presence of mind, is greater than the importance of observing specific details of physical posture and gesture during recital. It

is these concerns of inward conviction that are the consistent, common emphasis of the hadiths studied here.

Bibliography

Al-Azharī, Muḥammad b. Aḥmad, *Tahdhīb al-lugha*, Beirut: Dār Iḥyā' al-Turāth al-ʿArabī, 1421/2001.

Al-Baḥrānī al-Iṣfahānī, ʿAbdullāh Nūr Allāh, *ʿAwālim al-ʿulūm wa-l-maʿārif wa-l-aḥwāl min al-āyāt wa-l-akhbār wa-l-aqwāl* (*Mustadrak Sayyidat al-Nisā' ilā al-Imām al-Jawād*), Qom: Mu'assasat al-Imām al-Mahdī, 1413/1992.

Al-Baghdādī, al-Khaṭīb Aḥmad b. ʿAlī, *Ta'rīkh Baghdād,* ed. Muṣṭafā ʿAbd al-Qādir ʿAṭā, Beirut: Dār al-Kutub al-ʿIlmiyya, 1417/1997.

Farāhīdī, Khalīl b. Aḥmad, *Kitāb al-ʿayn,* Qom: Intishārāt-i Hijrat, 1409/1998.

Al-Fayyūmī, Aḥmad b. Muḥammad, *al-Miṣbāḥ al-munīr fī gharīb al-Sharḥ al-kabīr lil-Rāfiʿī* (Qom: Dār al-Hijra, 1414/1993.

Al-Ḥillī, al-Ḥasan b. Yūsuf Ibn al-Muṭahhar, *Khulāṣat al-aqwāl,* ed. Muḥammad Ṣādiq Baḥr al-ʿUlūm, Najaf: Dār al-Dhakhā'ir, 1411/1990.

Ibn ʿAbbād, al-Ṣāḥib Abū l-Qāsim Ismāʿīl, *al-Muḥīṭ fī l-lugha,* ed. Muḥammad Ḥasan Āl Yāsīn, Beirut: ʿĀlam al-Kutub, 1414/1994.

Ibn al-Athīr, Al-Mubārak b. Muḥammad, *al-Nihāya fī gharīb al-ḥadīth wa-l-athar,* Qom: Mu'assasat Ismāʿīlīyān, 1367 Sh./1988.

Ibn Bābawayh, Muḥammad b. ʿAlī al-Shaykh al-Ṣadūq, *al-Amālī,* Tehran: Kitābchī, 1376 Sh./1997.

ʿUyūn akhbār al-Riḍā, Tehran: Intishārāt-i Jahān, 1378 Sh./1958.

Kamāl al-dīn wa-tamām al-niʿma, ed. ʿAlī Akbar Ghaffārī, Tehran: Dār al-Kutub al-Islāmiyya, 1395/1975.

Ibn Durayd, Muḥammad b. al-Ḥasan, *Jamharat al-lugha,* Beirut: np., 1988.

Ibn Fāris, Aḥmad, *Muʿjam maqāyīs al-lugha*, Qom: Maktab al-Iʿlām al-Islāmī, 1404/1983.

Ibn Manẓūr, Abū l-Faḍl Jamāl al-Dīn Muḥammad, *Lisān al-ʿArab*, Beirut: Dār Ṣādir, 1414/1993.

Ibn Ṭāwūs, Raḍī al-Dīn ʿAlī b. Mūsā, *al-Iqbāl bi-l-aʿmāl*, ed. Jawād Qayyūmī Iṣfahānī, Qom: Daftar-i Tablīghāt-i Islāmī, 1376 Sh./1997.

Jamāl al-usbūʿ bi-kamāl al-ʿamal al-mashrūʿ, Qom: Dār al-Raḍī, 1330/1911.

Al-Jawharī, Ismāʿīl b. Ḥammād, *al-Ṣiḥāḥ*, ed. Aḥmad ʿAbd al-Ghafūr ʿAṭṭār, Beirut: Dār al-ʿIlm lil-Malāyīn, 1376/1956.

Al-Kashshī, Muḥammad b. ʿUmar, *Ikhtiyār maʿrifat al-rijāl* (*Rijāl al-Kashshī*), ed. Ḥasan Muṣṭafawī, Mashhad: Muʾassasa-yi Nashr-I Dānishgāh-I Mashhad, 1409/1998.

Al-Khoei, Abū l-Qāsim, *Muʿjam rijāl al-ḥadīth wa tafṣīl tabaqāt al-ruwāt*, London: Muʾassasat al-Imām al-Khūʾī al-Islāmiyya, nd.

Kohlberg, Etan, *Kitābkhāna-yi Ibn-I Ṭāwūs wa aḥwāl wa āthār-I ū*, trans. Rasul Jafarian and ʿAlī Quli Qarai, Qom: Kitābkhāna-yi ʿUmūmī-yi Ḥaḍrat-I Āyatullāh al-ʿUẓmā Marʿashī Najafī, 1371 Sh./1992.

Al-Kulaynī, Muḥammad b. Yaʿqūb, *al-Kāfī*, Qom: Dār al-Ḥadīth, 1429/2008.

Al-Majlisī, Muḥammad Bāqir, *Biḥār al-anwār*, Beirut: Dār Iḥyāʾ al-Turāth al-ʿArabī, 1403/1983.

Zād al-maʿād wa miftāḥ al-jinān, ed. ʿAlāʾ al-Dīn al-Aʿlamī, Beirut: Muʾassasat al-Aʿlamī lil-Maṭbūʿāt, 1423/2002.

Al-Māmaqānī, ʿAbdullāh, *Tanqīḥ al-maqāl fī ʿilm al-rijāl*, np., nd.

Al-Muṣṭafawī, Ḥasan, *al-Taḥqīq fī kalimāt al-Qurʾān al-karīm* (Beirut, Cairo, London: Markaz Nashr Āthār al-ʿAllāma al-Muṣṭafawī, 1430/2008.

Noor Software (Muʾassasa-yi Taḥqīqāt-I Kāmpyūtirī-yi Nūr), *Tarājim wa kitābshināsī* 3.

Rijāl-I Shīʿa

Jāmiʿ al-aḥādīth

Majmūʿa-yi Āthār-I Sayyid Ibn Ṭāwūs

Qummī, ʿAbbās, *Mafātīḥ al-jinān*, Mashhad: Intishārāt-I Āstān-I Quds-I Raḍawī, 1379 Sh./2000.

Shāhrūdī, ʿAlī Namāzī, *Mustadrakāt ʿilm rijāl al-ḥadīth*, Tehran: Farzand-i Mu'allif, 1414/1993.

Shūshtarī, Muḥammad Taqī, *Qāmūs al-rijāl*, Qom: Mu'assasat al-Nashr al-Islāmī 1410/1989.

Tihrānī, Āqā Buzurg Muḥammad Muḥsin, *al-Dharīʿa ilā taṣānīf al-Shīʿa*, Beirut: Dār al-Aḍwā', 1403/1982.

Ṭabaqāt aʿlām al-Shīʿa, Beirut: Dār Iḥyā' al-Turāth al-ʿArabī, 1430/2008.

Al-Ṭurayḥī, Fakhr al-Dīn b. Muḥammad, *Majmaʿ al-baḥrayn*, Tehran: al-Maktaba al-Murtaḍawiyya, 1375 Sh./1996.

Al-Ṭūsī, Muḥammad b. al-Ḥasan, *al-Rijāl* (*Rijāl al-Ṭūsī*), ed. Jawād Qayyūmī Iṣfahānī, Qom: Mu'assasat al-Nashr al-Islāmī, 1373 Sh./1994.

Miṣbāḥ al-mutahajjid wa silāḥ al-mutaʿabbid, Beirut: Mu'assasat Fiqh al-Shīʿa, 1411/1990.

Al-Zabīdī, Muḥammad b. Muḥammad, *Tāj al-ʿarūs min jawāhir al-qāmūs*, Beirut: Dār al-Fikr, 1414/1993.

Al-Zamakhsharī, Maḥmūd b. ʿUmar, *Muqaddimat al-adab*, Tehran: Mu'assasa-yi Muṭālaʿāt-i Islāmī-yi Dānishgāh-i Tihrān, 1386 Sh./2007.

Al-Qalam Journal

BOOK REVIEWS

The Hundred Years' War on Palestine: A History of Settler Colonialism and Resistance, 1917-2017[1]

Written by Rashid Khalidi

Review by Mehdi Ali

Rashid Khalidi's account of the history of Palestine is a deeply moving and informative story about the plight of the Palestinians throughout the last century. Instead of merely regurgitating important historical, legal, and political developments, Khalidi provides poignant context that makes the story of Palestine feel profoundly personal. This context is drawn in part from his own experiences and family history, beginning with childhood memories of accompanying his father to various United Nations meetings, as well as bringing to life the memoirs and diary entries of his uncle, Hussein Khalidi, the former mayor of Jerusalem, who was exiled by Britain.

Khalidi's own career as a prominent voice in the West for the Palestinian cause also plays an important role in this story, including relaying anecdotes about negotiating on behalf of the Palestine delegation at various international forums, reporting on his meetings with Yasser Arafat and other well-known Palestinian leaders, and providing first-hand observations of the Israeli occupation and bombardment of Lebanon in the 1980s.

The book is divided into six main chapters (in addition to an introduction and conclusion), with each chapter exploring an important moment or period in Palestinian history. At each juncture, Khalidi demonstrates how Palestine and its people have been betrayed by its interlocutors.

The first chapter begins by describing life in Palestine before the

---

[1] Picador, 319, notes, index, ISBN 978-1-250-78765-1

creation of the State of Israel, including cultural features of the existing Mizrahi and Sephardic Jewish community. Khalidi describes how the demographics of the region began to shift rapidly after the advent of Zionism and the Balfour Declaration. The Balfour Declaration, despite being only a single sentence, was an especially momentous development because it meant that the Zionist project, which ignored the needs of the native Arabs who formed the overwhelming majority of the indigenous population, was now backed by the world's most powerful military force.

Khalidi does an excellent job of providing a sense of the mood at this time by exploring a variety of primary sources, including contemporary Arabic-language news accounts. This mood included intense political opposition to the Zionist movement, including the Arab revolt of 1936-1939 that was suppressed by the British. Khalidi argues that another momentous change occurred with the rise of Naziism in Germany, which facilitated unprecedented levels of Jewish immigration to Palestine.

The second chapter focuses on the creation of the State of Israel, which resulted in the displacement of over 700,000 Palestinians. Khalidi astutely documents Israel's ability to build relations with foreign governments and especially to appeal to foreign public opinion in places like the United States, which allowed for the Zionist mission to continue largely unencumbered. Conversely, Arab nations did not give due attention to the Palestinian cause, which allowed them to be further sidelined. In fact, they were often working in direct opposition to Palestinian interests, as evidenced by King Abdullah's negotiations with leaders of the Jewish Agency and his secret negotiations with the British. Khalidi notes that "the Palestinians had not developed effective Arab allies or the apparatus of a modern state."

Khalidi also notes that there were deep differences among the Palestinian leadership, which further hampered its cause. And perhaps most importantly, he believes that a severely limited grasp of global politics by Palestinian leadership was a big reason for the stunting of the Palestinian cause during this time. The chapter discusses the UN's recommendation to partition Palestine in 1947, which led to the Nakba, during which the ethnic cleansing of Palestine took place, transforming the demographic make-up of Palestine. The resulting Palestinian refugees faced harsh circumstances, many of which continue until today. The chapter also discusses the evolution of Israel's relationship with the United States.

The third chapter explores the Six Day War in 1967, and the ensuing crushing military defeat of the Egyptian, Syrian, and Jordanian armies. As a result of Israel's devastating first strike, which was aided by the actions of the United States, it was able to occupy the West Bank, Gaza Strip, Golan Heights, and Sinai Peninsula in short order. A key after-effect of this was Security Council Resolution 242, which "linked any Israel withdrawal to peace treaties with the Arab states and the establishment of secure frontiers." The resolution also had the benefit of "enlarged Israeli borders to meet the criterion of security, as determined by Israel" and to endorse the "1949 armistice lines (since known as the 1967 borders or the Green Line)" and thus "indirectly consenting to [Israel's] conquest of most of Palestine in the 1948 war."

Khalidi provides a highly nuanced perspective on the United States' changing policy toward Palestine and Israel during this time. Yet Khalidi also tells the story of how 1967 sparked a revival of the Palestinian movement, and gives details about some of the resistance organisations that were formed during this time. Most prominent is the story of the PLO, formed by the Arab League to control the resistance, although it often clashed with various Arab governments. Khalidi's description includes details regarding the evolution of the PLO's thinking, most importantly from advocating a single state to eventually accepting a two-state solution. Khalidi notes that "the Palestinian resurgence posed little or no threat to Israel in strategic terms ... [but] it constituted an entirely different kind of challenge on the discursive level, one that was existential." Khalidi also details the limited success of the Palestinian cause in diplomatic circles and in the United States.

The fourth chapter begins with the Israeli occupation of Lebanon, which was ostensibly initiated as a response to attacks by Palestinian militants in Lebanon, although, according to Khalidi, no PLO leaders were ever killed. The commentary in this chapter is especially interesting because Khalidi is narrating from a first-person perspective, including the many atrocities inflicted by Israel on the civilians of Lebanon, including the IDF-supported Sabra and Shatila refugee camp massacres. Khalidi also describes the support by the United States for the massacres that occurred after the Palestinian resistance had been expelled from Beirut.

The fifth chapter focuses on the First Intifada, the spontaneous Palestinian uprising that began in 1987 and lasted until 1995. Khalidi argues that the First Intifada did much to engender sympathy for the Palestinian cause. Khalidi also spends time discussing the problems with the PLO, whose exiled leadership failed to keep up with events in the Occupied Territories. Furthermore, the PLO "allowed itself to be drawn into a process explicitly designed by Israel, with the acquiescence of the United States, to prolong its occupation and colonization, not to end them."

The parts where Khalidi is critical of the PLO are arguably the most insightful parts of the book because he recognises the mistakes Palestinian leaders made which further harmed the Palestinian cause. The PLO made a series of missteps, including supporting Iraq in its invasion of Kuwait, which "made the organization a pariah among the Gulf states on which it depended for financial support." Khalidi also provides a first-hand account of the political negotiations that took place in Madrid, including the important players from the US and Israeli sides. Further, he astutely analyses the Oslo Accords, which were disastrous from the Palestinian perspective.

The sixth chapter discusses developments since the beginning of the twenty-first century, including the continued colonisation of the West Bank and parts of East Jerusalem, which eventually led to the Second Intifada. He also describes the emergence of Hamas as a formidable rival in an atmosphere of widespread dissatisfaction with the current Palestinian leadership. Khalidi argues that the Second Intifada was a "major setback for the Palestinian national movement" because it led to Israel's reoccupation of areas that had been "evacuated as part of the Oslo Accords."

Khalidi argues that the Second Intifada was a public relations failure, as it weakened the sympathy that had been garnered by the Palestinian people. Khalidi describes other developments as well, including Hamas's control of Gaza, Israel's subsequent siege and other military incursions, and the indifference of the US, if not outright support, of Israel's repression of the Palestinians.

This book is a very useful and necessary history of Palestine over the last hundred years. Although Khalidi certainly provides a perspective sympathetic to Palestinians, he is by no means uncritical of the decisions of the Palestinian leadership. He is fully aware that many mistakes were made over the course of the century, including an inability to overcome internal divisions among the leadership. Thus, in addition to being an indictment of Zionism and settler colonialism, this book is also a powerful rebuke to the Palestinian leadership. The reader is left to surmise that perhaps the history of Palestine could have been very different with a more sophisticated and selfless group of leaders.

Khalidi also highlights the role of the United States in preventing a resolution to the Palestine question, a country that likes to present itself as a neutral arbiter but that has done much damage to the efforts to create a fair solution to the conflict.

In the conclusion, Khalidi recognises that one of the resounding successes of Zionism has been its ability to create a powerful national identity. Thus, he refuses to indulge the incredulity of many Arabs, who are unwilling to acknowledge that modern-day Israelis feel a deep nationalistic connection to their country. Instead, he offers a thoughtful vision for the future, where both sides must learn to coexist, and to acknowledge each other's reality on the ground, if there is any chance for peace in the Middle East.

A Short History of Islamic Thought[1]

Written by Fitzroy Morrisey

Review by George Warner

Fitzroy Morrissey's A History of Islamic Thought addresses itself to a non-academic audience, setting out across 200-odd eminently readable pages the key concepts, individuals, and movements that have shaped Muslim intellectual traditions over the past 1400 years. Twelve chapters take the reader from Islam's origins through to the modernist experiments of the twentieth century, followed by a brief epilogue that brings the book's account into conversation with the present moment. Though the continued, sometimes urgent relevance of the history he narrates is made clear, Morrissey is also careful to affirm that the systems of thought here described are of great value in and of themselves, as vital and venerable records of human interrogation of the profound questions of existence.

That Morrissey manages to narrate the history of such complex material while retaining pace and lucidity is no mean feat. His approach is largely descriptive rather than analytical, forgoing lengthy examinations of impersonal forces and theories to focus instead upon individual figures of significance, deftly introducing the big ideas through (usually) miniature intellectual biographies of their chief proponents. The early debates about the derivation of the law, and with them the fundamental dynamics of balancing reason and revelation, are narrated through the scholarly careers of the four Imams of the Sunnī madhāhib, while the life of Ibn ʿAbd al-Wahhāb is used to introduce principal beliefs of what later became Salafism. Morrissey's account is further enlivened by the integration of Muslim voices into his assessment of different developments. Historians like Ibn Khallikān

---

[1] Apollo, 256 pages, bibliography, notes, ISBN: 978-1-789-54566-1

and Ibn Khaldūn are cited for their insights on events many centuries before their births, while the French occupation of Egypt is described chiefly through the testimonies of Egyptians who witnessed it.

An important success of the book is its balancing of attention between different historical periods. While introductory works on Islam often dwell on a designated "formative" period around the Abbasid era, before leapfrogging the throng of societies that flourished thereafter to arrive at European colonialism, Morrissey's history follows the continued unfolding of intellectual trends and systems across the centuries. The challenge of Islam's immense and geographically dispersed diversity is similarly well managed. Not only are good accounts made of different centres of learning from Cordoba to Delhi, but Morrissey illustrates the constant exchange of ideas across vast distances that characterises Islamic history, from the hostile reception of al-Ghazālī's works in Islamic Spain to the influence in Ottoman lands of a Ḥanafī fiqh manual commissioned by a Mughal sultan.

Morrissey points out early on that most Muslims for most of history have been Sunnī, and correspondingly focuses on Sunnī thinkers, but here again the book keeps a balance, and Shīʿī intellectual currents are kept in sustained conversation with the broader narrative. Naṣīr al-Dīn al-Ṭūsī's philosophical theology is introduced alongside that of his Sunnī counterparts, and the debates between Akhbārīs and Uṣūlīs are juxtaposed with scripturalist and revivalist movements within the Ottoman milieu. Indeed, another strength of the book is the care taken to alert the reader to connections and continuities between the manifold facets of the subject matter, tracking the posthumous influence of figures like al-Ghazālī and Ibn Taymiyya, as well as the recurrent importance of concepts like taqlīd, shirk, and the Mahdī. The latter feature is facilitated by the author's readiness to introduce technical terms from the relevant languages, and terms and names alike are meanwhile transliterated impeccably.

The book's most consequential choices of emphasis concern its framing as a history not of Islam in general but specifically of Islamic thought. Accordingly, the bulk of the book is devoted to religious thinkers and their associated institutions, while the historical events that surrounded them are given significantly less airtime than in other, comparable works. Discussion of such seismic changes as the Mongol invasions is kept to the bare minimum necessary for clarity, and even the foundational narratives of the Prophet's life are passed over somewhat briefly, though not to the exclusion of the hermeneutical puzzles that they presented in later centuries. This is nothing less than what the book declares itself to be doing, although occasionally, as when the narrative jumps straight from the policies of ʿUmar b. al-Khaṭṭāb to the Abbasid miḥna, the pace may test uninitiated readers.

At the heart of the book is Morrissey's excellent account of the development of Muslim philosophical theology. Swiftly quashing outdated stereotypes of al-Ghazālī's elimination of philosophy in the fifth/eleventh century, he sets out across four chapters a careful account of the continued prominence, relevance, richness, and development of the synthesis between Ashʿarī kalām, Avicennan logic, and the Ṣūfī metaphysics of Ibn ʿArabī. Encompassing, as usual, a plurality of historical contexts, the book is especially detailed in this domain, taking in, inter alia, Ibn Rushd's Aristotelian turn and the Ottoman-era entente between Ashʿarī and Māturīdī kalām.

Readers are especially well served here by Morrissey's skilful exposition of the axial concepts at work, from Ṣūfī discourses of fanāʾ to Ibn Sīnā's proof of God as the Necessary Being (wājib al-wujūd). A recurring point of attention, meanwhile, is the sustained intellectual prominence of philosophical-theological traditions, be it in the regnal ideologies of sultans or through the continued presence of these traditions in the curricula of institutions of learning. This is not generally a book that makes explicit arguments, but here one has a clear sense of Morrissey making the case for the ongoing centrality of these grand systems of thought in Muslim intellectual life into the modern period.

This portion of the book is also surely its most valuable. While there is no shortage of popular works concerning Islam's origins and/

or its modern iterations, books introducing Fakhr al-Dīn al-Rāzī and his commentators to the general reader are a rarer phenomenon, let alone those with authors possessing a proper understanding of the subject, and Morrissey's contribution is an especially welcome one on both counts. Though not presented as an undergraduate textbook, it at least matches the quality of many such works, and deserves a place on university reading lists in addition to its appeal beyond the classroom.

As a whole, A Short History of Islamic Thought is accurate, informative, and well balanced. Endnotes refer readers to a solid range of up-to-date secondary literature, and factual errors are very rare (al-Sharīf al-Murtaḍā's office of naqīb, for example, marked him as representative of the descendants of ʿAlī, not of the Twelver Shīʿī community as Morrissey states). If complaints are to be justly directed at such a work, they should be accompanied by suggestions of how extra material might have been accommodated without disrupting the necessary brevity and symmetry that Morrissey's account achieves. While one might very well lament the absence of the Sokoto caliphate or of al-Jāḥiẓ, one might, nevertheless, stop short of insisting that their inclusion should take the place of some existing component of the book.

Forging ahead in spite of this caveat, a thematic point that does deserve interrogation concerns the author's inevitable decisions regarding what constitutes Islamic thought. Part of this rests on definitions of the "religious"; pursuits that have occupied myriad Muslim thinkers over the centuries, but which are sometimes classed as extraneous to religion in other contexts, such as linguistics and literatures of manners (adab), are seldom mentioned, presumably for such reasons of taxonomy. Similarly, the slippery continuum between religious and political discourses engenders a coverage that can look uneven, with the dynamics of imperial power at work in the Ottoman, Safavid, and Mughal empires receiving far more attention than those operating in earlier polities.

A further, more significant dimension of how Islamic thought is defined concerns the delineation of where Muslims have been at their most thoughtful. Though, as noted above, this is not a book that makes many overt arguments, the weighting of its contents makes fairly clear that it is in the work of figures like Fakhr al-Dīn al-Rāzī and Ṣadr al-Dīn al-Qūnawī that Morrissey locates Islamic thought's centre of gravity. His account of this tradition is a very fine one, but this focus does divert attention from other aspects of Muslim intellectual life over the centuries, aspects wherein, I would suggest, Muslim thinkers have been no less ingenious. Morrissey allots space to hadith scholars, to religious law, and to messianic movements, but such domains are not treated in the same depth as are metaphysical matters.

The sophisticated debates of Islamic jurisprudence regarding the nature of certainty, for instance, are not discussed, nor is much attention given to such core animating questions as why the legislative aspect of revelation (and with it the sharīʿa) were and remain so important, what kinds of encounter with the past and with history are enacted in hadith literature, and why a religion founded on the finality of its prophet often appears so interested in messiah figures.

It may be objected that such questions are less explicit in the source material than the enquiries of philosophers, and would thus require a different, perhaps less accessible kind of book. Regardless, their absence affects not just an editorial choice but a consequential evaluation of the subject matter.

The Caliph and the Imam, The Making of Sunnism and Shiism[1]

Written by Toby Matthiesen

Review by Syed A.H. Zaidi, Fordham University

Toby Matthiesen's The Caliph and the Imam is an important contribution to the field of Twelver Shīʿī studies. It is a voluminous work of over 700 pages with extensively long footnotes which covers the Sunnī-Shīʿī divide in the Islamic world from the death of Prophet Muḥammad (d. 11/632) until the present day. He argues that the 1400 year conflict has been politically motivated by policies that Muslim leaders set throughout the centuries. It examines how intra-faith and interfaith debates were motivated by dialogues between various tribes, nations, empires, and modern states. One of the great strengths of this book is the fact that it attempts to be interdisciplinary by nature. In other words, Matthiesen examines the conflict from a historical, anthropological, sociological, and religious studies approach. The book is divided into four parts. Due to the size of the work, it is impossible to provide a complete summary.

The first part examines the beginning of the division of the Muslim community from after the death of Prophet Muḥammad and the early caliphate (11/632-41/661). It examines the Shīʿī position regarding the caliphate which claims that ʿAlī ibn Abī Ṭālib (d. 41/661) and the family of the Prophet (Ahl al-Bayt) were ignored or repressed during the selection of Abū Bakr (d. 13/634), ʿUmar (d. 24/644), and ʿUthmān (d. 36/656). However, all of these narratives primarily come out of Shīʿī narratives and do not include the Sunnī position regarding these issues.

The first sentence of this section begins with the phrase, "According to Muslim tradition ..." as if all Muslim scholars are in agreement with

---

[1] Oxford University Press. xv+731, bibliography, index. ISBN 978-0190689469

the nature of the birth, life, and death of Prophet Muḥammad, and the events which came after that.

With this said, Matthiesen constantly claims to be presenting both the Shīʿī and Sunnī positions of what happened. However, the narrative reads as if he is presenting the Sunnī narrative (when he brings it in) as a response to the Shīʿī narrative.

Furthermore, from the beginning, Matthiesen never critically examines the historical sources which he narrates from. For example, he cites from al-Ṭabarī (d. 311/923), but does not mention whether al-Ṭabarī was a Sunnī or Shīʿī historian. Although most sources claim that he was a Jarīrī, some claim that he may have been a Shīʿī Muslim. Furthermore, al-Ṭabarī very rarely leaves a moment of history without critical examination. This would have made him as much a historiographer as a historian.

It is surprising that this book does not mention this important fact.

Throughout this section, there are important religious narratives that were not mentioned. For example, Matthiesen writes that the famous sword of ʿAlī ibn Abī Ṭālib, known as Dhū al-Faqār, "belonged to a Meccan who was killed in a fight against the Muslims at the Battle of Badr in 3/624. Thereafter, it is believed to have been one of the swords of the Prophet, who gave it to ʿAlī during the battle of Uḥud of the same year." This is a very contested report amongst both the Sunnī and Shīʿa. Many Muslims actually argue that this sword was a gift from the Prophet which he received from heaven. Regardless of the historical reality, it would have been important for Matthiesen to mention that all of these religious artifacts have disputed origins and inform different narratives throughout the centuries.

One of the most problematic parts of this section is the fact that the Ṣūfis are almost never mentioned when it comes to the 2nd/8th eighth centuries, respectively. In the first section, Matthiesen addresses the important figures who founded the four schools of Sunnī law and early Shīʿī figures. But he never mentions Ḥasan al-Baṣrī (d. 110/728), al-Ḥārith al-Muḥāsibī (d. 243/857), and other early figures. Being prominent Sunnī mystics, these are all figures who either influenced Sunnī positions on the family of the Prophet, or were in direct contact with the family and therefore had their own positions, which may have also influenced Shīʿī portrayals of the family of the Prophet. Despite this, Matthiesen still adequately covers major aspects of how the first centuries of Islam created the leavens of the dispute between the two largest groups of Muslims.

The second section examines how various Muslim empires dealt with the dispute within their polities. One of the greatest sections of this part is the fact that it was much more inclusive of the various groups of Islam, which informed the Sunnī-Shīʿī narratives and disputes. For example, this section begins with an examination of how the Safavid dynasty's Ṣūfī origins influenced how they dealt with different forms of Ṣūfī orders. For examples, they were antagonistic towards Sunnī Ṣūfīs, but were sympathetic to what he calls Shīʿī Ṣūfī orders.

However, certain glaring mistakes cause one to wonder whether proper research was done with respect to the shrine culture in Iran. For example, Matthiesen writes that there was a shrine built in honour of the murderer of ʿUmar. However, unlike other shrines which he examines, he fails to mention that this shrine was a major site of pilgrimage for Persian Shīʿī Muslims until very recently. In his discussion of the Friday prayer, Matthiesen never mentions the fact that the famous Shīʿī philosopher and jurist, Mīr Dāmād (d. 1031/1631), was essential in re-mandating this prayer for all Shīʿī Muslims. Nonetheless, his discussions on the relations between the gunpowder empires and other empires, and the role of these relationships with respect to Shīʿī-Sunnī polemics, remains groundbreaking.

The last two sections continue to address how the age of colonialism and post-colonialisation informs the ongoing Sunnī-Shīʿī crises. Matthiesen's discussion of how regional powers in the Middle East informed the crises between the Sunnī and Shīʿa is essential to any course on modern Islamic political thought. Furthermore, he demonstrates how many of these powers have been able to invoke historical imagery to bolster their own religious narratives and policies. Matthiesen accurately analyses how Shīʿī and Sunnī religious leaders have been able to inform religious feelings and thought in South Asia in a manner which is rarely found.

The Caliph and the Imam is a welcome addition to the study of Islam. Many sections of this book are useful for courses such as an "Introduction to Islamic Political Thought" or even "Introduction to Islam". However, the work could have been improved by including narratives from early Ṣūfī and philosophical figures.

Also, although Matthiesen writes that he approaches this work from a religious studies perspective, he never introduces any modern or critical theorists to his approach to Sunnī or Shīʿī narratives. Surely, concepts such as Michel Foucault's archive could have been used in how he understood hadith narratives of both groups.

Furthermore, although this is not due to any fault of the author, this work required proper copy-editing. For example, the entire work lacks proper spaces between periods (.) and subsequent sentences. Also, there is inconsistency with respect to the use of Islamic calendar dates throughout the work. Nonetheless, this work is an important contribution to the study of Shiism and Sunnism.

Al-Qalam Journal

NEWS AND ANNOUNCEMENTS

ICAIR Announces the Appointment of its Governing Board

The International Centre for Advanced Islamic Research (ICAIR) is proud to announce the appointment of its governing board, a significant milestone in its journey.

ICAIR aims to address the intellectual and ethical challenges facing the KSIMC and the global Shīʿa community by bridging the divide between the community, the seminaries, and universities, and making scholarship on Shīʿī Islam accessible to all. This esteemed group, composed of distinguished scholars and professionals, will play a pivotal role in shaping the future of ICAIR.

The ICAIR Governing Board's primary role is to provide strategic direction and oversight, ensuring that ICAIR's activities align with its mission and objectives. This includes guiding the research agenda, overseeing major projects, and ensuring fiscal responsibility. The board will also work closely with the Head of ICAIR, offering support and advice to enhance the institute's operations and impact.

With a blend of expertise in Islamic studies, academia, and strategic development, the board members bring a wealth of knowledge and experience. Their guidance will be instrumental in steering ICAIR's initiatives, from academic research and publications to seminars, workshops, and public outreach programmes.

On 14 October 2023, the ICAIR Governing Board convened its first meeting. The session focused on defining ICAIR's strategic vision and establishing a detailed development plan. Key areas of academic research, community engagement, and operational growth were discussed, setting a clear direction for the institute's future endeavours.

The list of appointed members to the ICAIR Governing Board is as follows:

Chairman: Alhaj Safder Jaffer, President of The World Federation of KSIMC

Arifali Hirji, Secretary General of The World Federation of KSIMC

Shaykh Murtadha Alidina, Head of Islamic Education at The World Federation of KSIMC

Sayyid Sulayman Hassan, President and Religious Director of Imam-e Asr Islamic Seminary

Professor Cyrus Zargar, Al-Ghazali Distinguished Professor of Islamic Studies at the University of Central Florida

Professor Aun Hasan Ali, Assistant Professor in the Department of Religious Studies at CU Boulder

Shan Hassam, Community Representative, Birmingham, UK

Al-Qalam Journal

CALL FOR PAPERS

ICAIR Conference 2024: Call for Papers

"God in the Modern World"

Annual Conference of the

International Centre *for* Advanced Islamic Research

Friday 19th April – Sunday 21st April 2024

Jaffari Community Centre, Toronto

"... we need to think about Islamic tradition as a way of asking questions that cut across (and transgress) the assumptions of a purely secular world ..."

- Talal Asad

In the contemporary world, the convergence of secularism, postmodernism, technological evolution, and scientific discovery poses significant challenges to traditional religious beliefs and the understanding of God:

- **Secularism's** push for separating religion from state and reducing its public influence demands that believers reconcile their faith with a predominantly rationalist and empirical societal framework.
- **Postmodernism's** scepticism towards absolute truths, questions the certainty and universal applicability of religious doctrines.
- **Technological advancements**, particularly in digital communication, transform how religious practices and community interactions are conducted, bringing into focus the authenticity of virtual spiritual experiences.
- **Scientific breakthroughs**, in fields like cosmology and biology, challenge traditional religious narratives about life and the universe, compelling an assessment of religious doctrines in

light of modern scientific understanding.

These challenges necessitate an ongoing, interdisciplinary dialogue to comprehend and articulate the role of God in an increasingly complex and diverse global landscape.

Against the backdrop of these debates, the International Centre for Advanced Islamic Research (ICAIR) welcomes submissions for the 2024 ICAIR Annual International Conference on topics related to, but not limited to:

1. The concept of God in contemporary Islamic theology and philosophy
2. Comparative perspectives on God in Abrahamic faiths
3. The Problem of Evil and other objections to theism
4. The role of spirituality in a technologically advanced world
5. Ethical and moral implications of modernity in understanding God
6. God in the arts and popular culture
7. The influence of globalization on perceptions of God
8. Scientific advancements and theological responses
9. Secularism, atheism, and faith in the 21st century
10. Educational approaches to teaching about God in modern contexts
11. Building religious communities in a secular age

While the broad focus of the conference is Islamic theology, we welcome perspectives from all faith and philosophical perspectives.

Submission Guidelines

- We welcome submissions from scholars, researchers, and thought leaders. We strongly encourage submissions from doctoral and early career researchers.
- Bursaries covering travel and accommodation are available on application.
- Please submit a 300 word abstract plus a 250 word biography via

online form at www.icair.ac/conference

Important Dates

1. Abstract submission deadline: Friday 8th March 2024.
2. Notification of acceptance: 22nd March 2024.

Participation and Attendance

The conference is open to scholars, students, as well as the general public. Details for registration and attendance will be provided closer to the date.

For further enquiries, please contact conference@icair.ac

About ICAIR

Established in 2021 by the World Federation of the KSIMC, the International Centre for Advanced Islamic Research (ICAIR) is committed to advancing the study of Shi'i Islam in the 21st Century. ICAIR aims to address the intellectual and ethical challenges facing the KSIMC and the global Shi'a community, by combining the depth of traditional seminary education with innovative academic research. At its core, the Centre is committed to pioneering research in the realm of Islamic studies, making its findings accessible through various avenues, including publications, lectures, courses, and notably, its bi-annual journal, al-Qalam ('the Pen').

Printed in Great Britain
by Amazon

42008683R00069